Nicole Franken

Corporate Responsibility in the clothing industry

From a consumer's perspective

Summary

This master's thesis aims to shed light on the consumer's perception of garment manufacturers that act responsibly and sustainably. Corporate Responsibility (CR) is an umbrella term encompassing the voluntary activities of companies that demonstrate their ethical and responsible behaviour. CR plays a significant role in modern business practice.

Although clothing has many functions such as protection and expression of individualism, social situation and attitude, its production causes massive harm to people and the natural environment.

This research focuses on the clothing industry and the impact of manufacturing, CR, the role of CR in business and the communication of CR in order to answer the following questions: What criteria determine socially responsible and sustainable behaviour according to German consumers' perceptions of fashion labels, which fashion labels are perceived as socially responsible and sustainable by the German consumer and through which communication measures do fashion labels achieve a socially responsible and sustainable reputation?

Empirically, the research is based on a qualitative research design approach. The findings of an online survey of 504 German women between 15 and 49 years of age are aligned with the opinions of seven experts who were interviewed.

The results show that the three most important criteria that determine the consumer's perception of socially responsible and sustainable behaviour of clothing companies are firstly good working conditions, secondly environmentally friendly production and thirdly an absence of chemicals or harmful substances in clothing.

The five most often mentioned fashion labels that are perceived as committed to CR are hessnatur, C&A, H&M, Tchibo and Esprit. Apart from that, shop, website and TV are the three most often mentioned channels in the survey, through which the interviewed women learned about the CR activities of fashion labels. Finally, the research reveals that communication of CR in Germany needs to be improved.

Zusammenfassung

Kleidung hat viele Funktionen; sie schützt vor Wind und Wetter, ist Ausdruck von Individualismus und sozialer Stellung. Allerdings verursacht ihre Herstellung enorme Schäden an Mensch und Umwelt.

Es gibt Unternehmen, die dem entgegenwirken und Verantwortung demonstrieren, sowohl aus sozialer Sicht, als auch durch nachhaltiges Handeln. Freiwillige Aktivitäten dieser Art werden unter dem Sammelbegriff Corporate Responsibility (CR) oder unternehmerische Verantwortung zusammengefasst. CR spielt mittlerweile eine wichtige Rolle im Wirtschaftskontext.

Diese Masterarbeit verfolgt das Ziel, mehr Kenntnis über die Wahrnehmung von Verbrauchern hinsichtlich sozial verantwortlichem und nachhaltigem Verhalten von Kleidungsherstellern zu gewinnen. Sie beleuchtet die Kleidungsindustrie und ihre produktionsbedingten Auswirkungen, den Begriff CR, die Rolle von CR in der Geschäftswelt sowie CR-Kommunikation. Dabei sollen folgende Fragen beantwortet werden:

Welche Kriterien bestimmen für deutsche Verbraucher sozial verantwortliches und nachhaltiges Verhalten? Welche Kleidermarken werden als sozial verantwortlich und nachhaltig wahrgenommen? Und durch welche Kommunikationsmaßnahmen erscheinen Kleidungshersteller als sozial verantwortlich und nachhaltig?

Empirisch basiert die Arbeit auf einem qualitativen Forschungsdesign. Die Ergebnisse einer bundesweiten Online-Befragung von 504 Frauen wurden mit den Meinungen von sieben Experten aus der Kleidungsindustrie oder dem Bereich CR abgeglichen. Demnach sind für die befragten Verbraucherinnen die drei wichtigsten Kriterien für ein sozial verantwortliches und nachhaltiges Verhalten von Kleidungsherstellern: Erstens gute Arbeitsbedingungen, zweitens umweltfreundliche Produktion und an dritter Stelle schadstofffreie Kleidung.

Die fünf meistgenannten Kleidungsmarken, die als unternehmerisch verantwortlich wahrgenommen werden, sind hessnatur, C&A, H&M, Tchibo und Esprit. Die drei meistgenannten Kanäle, durch welche die interviewten Verbraucherinnen von den CR-Aktivitäten der Kleidungsmarken erfuhren, sind das Ladenlokal, die Website und das Fernsehen. Neben diesen Erkenntnissen zeigt die Arbeit deutlich auf, dass CR-Kommunikation in Deutschland verbesserungswürdig ist.

Table of Contents

List of Abbreviations

AG | Aktiengesellschaft (German stock company)

Approx. | approximately

ATC | Agreement on textile and clothing

e.V. | eingetragener Verein (German registered association)

Ed. (Eds.) | Editor (Editors)

et al. | Et alii (Latin, meaning 'and others')

EU | European Union

EUR | Euro

CEO | Chief Executive Officer

CERES | Coalition for Environmentally Responsible Economics

CO2 | Carbon dioxide

CR | Corporate Responsibility

CSR | Corporate Social Responsibility

DIN | Deutsches Institut für Normierung
    (German Institute for Standardisation)

FLO | Fair-trade Labelling Organizations International e.V.

GATT | General Agreement on Tariffs and Trade

GOTS | Global Organic Textile Standard

GRI | Global Reporting Initiative

Ibid. | Ibidem (Latin, literally meaning, in the aforementioned place)

ILO | International Labour Organization

IVN | Internationaler Verband der Naturtextilwirtschaft e.V.
    (International Association of Natural Textile Industry)

KbA | Kontrolliert biologischer Anbau (Controlled organic cultivation)

KbT | Kontrolliert biologische Tierhaltung
    (Controlled biologically animal husbandry)

LTA | Long-Term Arrangement regarding international trade in Cotton

MFA | Multifibre Agreement

MRSL | Manufacturing Restricted Substances List

p. (pp.) | Page (pages)

POS | Point of Sale

STA | Short Term Arrangement
TBL | Triple Bottom Line
TCI | Textile and Clothing Industry
UNEP | United Nations Environment Programme
ZDHC | Zero Discharge of Hazardous Chemicals Programme

List of Tables

List of Figures

1 INTRODUCTION

1.1 Background and problem definition

Every human being needs clothing. This fact makes the textile and clothing industry (TCI) one of the largest in the world (GRIES, VEIT & WULFHORST 2014). Additionally, clothing is a status symbol. As the old saying goes, 'clothes maketh the man', clothing is an expression of individualism, social situation and attitude (ENGELHARDT 2012).

Most clothes sold in Europe are produced in a developing or emerging country for cost reasons (STARMANNS 2010). In such countries, clothes manufacturing does massive harm to both people and the environment because of the lack of regulations; too often we hear media reports of accidents that happen due to abusive working conditions such as the collapsed Rana Plaza building in Bangladesh with many dead and injured (BURCKHARDT 2013).

Simultaneously, environmental and social problems are among the greatest challenges facing us today and into the future (BUND, BROT FÜR DIE WELT & EVANGELISCHER ENTWICKLUNGSDIENST 2009; DUONG DINH 2010). In recent years, the concept of corporate responsibility has found its way onto the agendas of many companies (MAY 2011) and has become a normal part of success-oriented corporate communication (MAST 2013). On the one hand, because companies are powerful actors that verifiably cause environmental and social problems (CRANE & MATTEN 2010), a fact that is known to consumers, and on the other hand, due to the influence of CR on marketing goals such as customer loyalty (KOTLER ET AL. 2012) and reputation (IVEY 2007). In other words, CR has become of strategic use in business (GASTINGER & GAGGL 2015).

According to a poll, 82 per cent of the German population could not name a company that stands for environmental and climate protection while taking social concerns into account (WILLMROTH 2012). This ignorance shows the enormous need for appropriate CR communication (HEINRICH & SCHMIDPETER 2013).

1.2 Research objectives and questions

Against the background of the context presented above, the main aim of this master's thesis is to identify which clothing manufacturers are perceived as socially responsible and sustainable by the German consumer, how they have achieved this perception and which communication measures best convey their socially responsible and sustainable committment.

These aims lead to the following three research questions:

1) *What criteria determine socially responsible and sustainable behaviour according to German consumers' perceptions of fashion labels?*
2) *Which fashion labels are perceived as socially responsible and sustainable by the German consumer?*
3) *Through which communication measures do clothing companies achieve a socially responsible and sustainable perception?*

This research focuses on Germany and German consumers.

1.3 Research structure

Chapter one, the introduction, opens up into the topic of the research, explains the research objectives and questions and gives an overview of the research content.

The literature review in the second chapter provides information on the theme of the master's thesis and of topics strongly related to it. The second chapter also discusses the textile and clothing industry and gives a detailed overview of various facets of corporate responsibility; the historical background, definitions of terms, CR in practice, the role of CR in business, and its extent in the TCI.

Chapter three describes the methodology used in the research in order to provide answers to the research questions and objectives. Chapter four deals with the research findings that are discussed in chapter five. Chapter six lays down the conclusions of the research and chapter seven contains an outlook.

2 LITERATURE REVIEW

Although the research questions focus on the clothing industry, in the following literature review much of the data refers to the textile and clothing industry as a whole, because specific data solely about the clothing industry is not available.

2.1 Textile and clothing industry

2.1.1 Economic significance

After the telecommunications, the chemical and the automotive industries, the TCI is the fourth-largest industry in the world (GRIES, VEIT & WULFHORST 2014). German textile and clothing manufacturers alone have an expected revenue of EUR 17.5 billion in 2016 (STATISTA 2016). Additionally, the TCI is the second largest consumer goods industry in Germany after the food sector. As an economic factor within the German national economy, however, the medium-sized German TCI is of comparably low significance. Nevertheless, many jobs in Germany in other industries depend directly or indirectly on the German TCI, such as engineering, the chemical industry, and the automotive industry (BUNDESMINISTERIUM FÜR WIRTSCHAFT UND ENERGIE 2016). This becomes more comprehensible when the role of technical textiles within the TCI in Germany is explained. The percentage share of turnover in the TCI accounted for by technical textiles is about 50 per cent; ten years ago that share was about one third. Abroad, the share of turnover represented by technical textiles is smaller (DEUTSCHE BANK RESEARCH 2011). Because of its flexibility and innovative strength, the German textile industry was able to strengthen its market position and increase the export rate of technical textiles, making Germany the world's leading exporter of technical textiles with exports of approx. EUR 7.1 billion in 2015 (BUNDESMINISTERIUM FÜR WIRTSCHAFT UND ENERGIE 2016; EULER HERMES ECONOMIC RESEARCH 2014). Moreover, German textile machine engineering is a world leader and has the highest export rate of all engineering industries in Germany (GRIES 2006).

However, the majority of clothing sold in Germany is not produced in Germany. Simultaneously the number of employees in the textile and clothing industry in Germany declined from approx. 500,000 at the beginning of 1990 to approx. 150,000 in 2005 (BECKERT 2014; BÜNDNIS FÜR NACHHALTIGE TEXTILIEN 2016; GRIES 2006; HAAS & ZADEMACH 2005; WILLERSHAUSEN 2012). In total, from 1970 to the present day, the German TCI has lost about 90 per cent of all its companies and employees (BUNDESMINISTERIUM FÜR WIRTSCHAFT UND ENERGIE 2016).

2.1.2 Structural change

There are three main reasons for this lasting structural change within the TCI in Germany since 1970 (GRÖMLING & MATTHES 2003; BUNDESMINISTERIUM FÜR WIRTSCHAFT UND ENERGIE 2016):

1) *Progress in productivity*
2) *Globalisation and expired trade restrictions*
3) *Changing consumer demand*

In the following, the three main aspects are explained:

1) Progress in productivity
Economic sectors with the highest increase in productivity lose significance in sectoral structural change. This means, the more productive a sector, the greater its loss of importance with regard to macroeconomic employment and the nominal value added (GRÖMLING & MATTHES 2003). This explains the low significance of the TCI as an economic factor in Germany, despite its being the second largest consumer goods industry in Germany.

2) Globalisation and expired trade restrictions
In the area of textile and clothing, there was a shift from the industrialised countries to the developing countries in terms of the worldwide value added and global trade. Since developing and emerging countries have a larger and cheaper unskilled workforce and less human- and real capital compared to industrialised countries, the production of very labour-intensive standard goods, such as textiles and clothing, by an unskilled workforce is much cheaper in those countries. Furthermore, other location factors relevant for the production costs are lower in developing and emerging countries, such as taxes and fees, working hours and machine running times; there is also less regulation. As early as the 1960s, compa-

nies from industrialised countries started establishing clothing factories in countries with lower labour costs (GRÖMLING & MATTHES 2003; DEUTSCHE BANK RESEARCH
2011).

Since the 1960s, the General Agreement on Tariffs and Trade (GATT) has regulated the international textile and clothing trade through trade restrictions, or 'special agreements'. The reason for these trade restrictions was the increased competition for the industrialised countries from developing and emerging countries.
High labour costs in the labour-intensive TCI increased competitive pressure for
high-wage countries such as the USA and the EU. In 1961, the very first agreement
for the TCI was reached, the Short Term Arrangement (STA), which was transformed into the Long-Term Arrangement Regarding International Trade in Cotton
Textiles (LTA) in 1962. The LTA was extended until 1973, by which time 40 countries had joined. It regulated trade with products made of cotton in the event of
a market disruption, such as when the imports of a country grew rapidly and the
prices of the exporting country were much lower than the prices of the importing
country. The Multifibre Agreement (MFA) replaced the LTA in 1974. 43 parties, including the EU, signed the MFA. In 1995, the Agreement on Textile and Clothing
(ATC) took the place of the MFA and every party that signed the ATC committed itself to terminating the regulations within ten years, i.e. by 2005. Globally,
the TCI was the most protected economic sector until the ATC was agreed. Many
parts of the TCI in industrialised countries only survived because of the intensive
protectionism since 1960. Free trade would have been their end (DEUTSCHE BANK
RESEARCH 2011; HAAS & ZADEMACH 2005; SCHNEIDER 2003).

3) Changing consumer demand
Long gone are the days when fashion houses put out two fashion collections per
year, summer and winter. Nowadays, consumers demand up to twelve collections
yearly, to meet their desire for pleasure, new experiences, status and identity
formation through buying clothes. 'Fast fashion' is the name of this phenomenon and it is an established economic term. Such garments are mass-produced,
standardized and cheap (EULER HERMES ECONOMIC RESEARCH 2014; FLETCHER 2014; HOL-
DINGHAUSEN 2015; ZERBACK 2015). 54 per cent of young people up to 17 years of age,
mostly young ladies, spend their pocket money on fashion, at a time, when they

have more money to spend than ever before (NUGGETS MARKET RESEARCH AND CON-
SULTING 2015; ZERBACK 2015). But this buyer group includes more than just adoles-
cents; a single adult woman buys 30 kilograms of clothes per year – a party-top
is worn 1.7 times on average before it is thrown away (EULER HERMES ECONOMIC
RESEARCH 2014; ZERBACK 2015). Fast fashion has the biggest market share in the TCI;
the consumption of clothing has increased by 400 per cent in the past two decades (AUST 2015).

2.1.3 Ecological impact

The textile and garment manufacturing industry has one of the longest and most
complicated production chains in the manufacturing industry and is recognised
as both a major user of water and a major polluter (FLETCHER 2014). A t-shirt sold in
Germany has already covered quite a distance before anyone wears it:

Harvest	Uzbekistan	0 km
Bleaching	Turkey	3,000 km
Weaving	China	7,000 km
Dying	Marocco	10,000 km
Creating T-shirt	Honduras	8,500 km
Printing	China	13,500 km
Labelling	Italy	8,000 km
Selling	Germany	600 km

Table 1: Production of a t-shirt sold in Germany.
Source: Adapted from Lux (2013).

The vast amount of resources consumed and the consequences of globalisation
with regard to CO_2 emissions and greenhouse gases show the absurdity of common production chains in the TCI (LUX 2013). Such production chains are standard
in today's economy because this is the cheapest way to produce garments price-
consciously for the end consumer (IBID.). The price is a critical aspect of fast fashion
and changed consumer demands as described in the previous section.

Due to price pressure, nearly all clothing that is available in Europe is produced in developing and emerging countries such as China, India, Bangladesh, Ukraine or Macedonia, to name a few (STARMANNS 2010). Because of incomplete or even a total lack of regulation and standards in these countries, the effects of globalised production chains cause massive harm to both people and the environment (BUND, BROT FÜR DIE WELT, & EVANGELISCHER ENTWICKLUNGSDIENST 2009). Cotton production is the root of one of the world's greatest ecological catastrophes; it is highly resource-consuming and chemical-intensive (FLETCHER 2014; BECKERT 2014). Cotton is, along with polyester, the most popular fiber in the clothing industry despite all the negative reports about its environmental impacts. The global cotton growing area has not changed significantly for around 80 years, but in that time the output has tripled, because of the use of large amounts of pesticides. Pesticides are a generic term incorporating insecticides, herbicides, and fungicides, with the latter accounting eleven per cent of global pesticide use (FLETCHER 2014). The cotton crop alone consumes one quarter of all insecticides used in agriculture worldwide (HOLDINGHAUSEN 2015). The water drawn down in the irrigation of the cotton crop can be up to 3,800 litres per kilogamme of cotton, depending on agricultural practices and climate (FLETCHER 2014). The Aral Sea in Uzbekistan, once the fourth largest lake on earth with 68,000 square kilometres, is now less than half its original size; the water volume is reduced by over 80 per cent. The reason is salinization, caused by the very water-intensive production of cotton. The intensive use of chemicals has resulted in dramatic illnesses within the population; they had to stop fishing here in the early 1990s. Today, the Aral Sea is considered biologically dead (ENGELHARDT 2012). Uzbekistan is the world's second largest cotton exporter (ENVIRONMENTAL JUSTICE FOUNDATION 2007). The Rio Grande in the USA and the Murray River in Australia (HOLDINGHAUSEN 2015) have suffered similarly but these are just a few examples of many that could be mentioned from across the planet.

2.1.4 Socio-economic impacts

Its disastrous ecological consequences, as described in the previous section, are not the only impact cotton production has had. Cotton is predominantly harvested by hand rather than by machine due to underinvestment in technology (CRANE & MATTEN 2010). Between 25 million and 77 million agricultural workers worldwide suffer from acute pesticide poisoning due to its use on cotton crops.

The symptoms include headaches, vomitting, tremors, lack of coordination, difficulty breathing or respiratory depression, loss of consciousness and death. In some countries such as Uzbekistan and India, children are directly involved in applying pesticides to cotton and in harvesting cotton (ENVIRONMENTAL JUSTICE FOUNDATION 2007; HOLDINGHAUSEN 2015). In 2008, after reporters unveiled forced child labour on a massive scale in Uzbekistan during the harvesting season, retailers such as Asda, Tesco, Marks and Spencer, H&M, Gap and Levi's signed a boycott of Uzbek cotton. As a consequence, the Uzbekistan government announced in the same year that it was to ban children under the age of 16 from picking cotton and signed International Labour Organization (ILO) conventions committing the country to stopping child labour. Given the poor record of the Uzbek authorities, people remain unconvinced that much will change however, which further reports of exploitation appear to back up (CRANE & MATTEN 2010, WILLIAMSON 2014).

In recent years, the media has revealed numerous scandals regarding production conditions in the TCI (WILLERSHAUSEN 2012). In September 2012, a clothing factory burned down in Pakistan; 300 people died. In November 2012, a clothing factory in Bangladesh burned; 112 people died. In April 2013, the Rana Plaza building in Bangladesh, another sweatshop (SCHERER 2007; HUWART & VERDIER 2014), collapsed; 1,127 people died, another 1,650 people were seriously injured. Thousands of people, men and women, fathers, mothers, and even children, lost arms, legs or their lives (BURCKHARDT 2013; BURCKHARDT 2014). Seamstresses in India, Ukraine, China, Macedonia, etc. work up to 16 hours a shift with barely a break; they work throughout the night, and for starvation wages. Workplace bullying and sexual assaults are not uncommon (BUNDESMINISTERIUM FÜR WIRTSCHAFTLICHE ZUSAMMENARBEIT UND ENTWICKLUNG 2015; BURKHARDT 2013; CLEAN CLOTHES CAMPAIGN 2014). In all the above cases, the factories were manufacturing clothing for European companies, among them many German ones (BURCKHARDT 2013).

Another example of inhumane working conditions involves denim, one of the most popular cloths for garment manufacturing in the world. Between two and three billion pairs of jeans are sold worldwide per year (HOLDINGHAUSEN 2015). Faded, worn-looking jeans are the latest must-have in the Western world and sandblasting is used to create this distressed look. In the process of sandblasting, compressors are used to blow out sand under pressure through thick hoses in order to bleach the denim. Workers holding the hoses are exposed to silica particles, which are tiny particles of blasted sand. Inhaled silica dust can cause severe respiratory problems for workers such as silicosis and lung cancer (CLEAN CLOTHING CAMPAIGN 2012). Turkey, once the main producer of sandblasted jeans, prohibited life-threatening sandblasting in 2009. According to the Turkish textile trade union, 700 deaths and 5,000 sufferers from respiratory illnesses have been recorded thus far.

Other methods such as laser beams have the same effect as sandblasting, but the investment required for them is expensive (HELL 2009; KOHN 2009; STIFTUNG WAREN-TEST 2011).

It is estimated that almost half of the 200 million pairs of jeans exported from Bangladesh each year are sandblasted. There are an estimated 2,000 full-time sandblasters here producing denim clothing for export (CLEAN CLOTHES CAMPAIGN 2012). Ominously, although one might think that the more a garment costs, the better its origin and quality, that is not the case. European fashion companies of all price ranges are buying from clothing factories producing under such conditions (CLEAN CLOTHES CAMPAIGN 2014).

2.2 Corporate Responsibility

The facts described above suggest that environmental and social problems are the greatest challenges facing us today and into the future (BUND, BROT FÜR DIE WELT & EVANGELISCHER ENTWICKLUNGSDIENST 2009; DUONG DINH 2010). Corporations are powerful social actors and verifiably cause ecological and social harm, among other things (CRANE & MATTEN 2010). Scandals such as Enron (RAPOPORT & DHARAN 2004), WorldCom, Parmalat, Lehman Brothers, and numerous others (VISSER 2013) contribute to the perception that corporations are unscrupulous because their aim is unlimited profit seeking. Accordingly, CR-issues have found their way onto the agendas of many companies in the past decade (MAY 2011). This makes it even more astonishing that no clear definition of the term CR exists. Quite to the contrary, there is a plethora of definitions set out in: Thousands of articles, reports, books, journals, and statements on CR from academics, corporations, consultancy firms, the media, NGOs and government departments (CRANE ET AL. 2008; CRANE, MATTEN & SPENCE 2014). In the following, the conceptual history of CR and its meaning is explained.

Although Corporate Social Responsibility (CSR) is the most common label for the actual topic, in this work the word 'social' has been deliberately omitted from this term in order to reflect the fact that not only social, but also ecological and key moral responsibilities are implied in this acronym, and 'social' matters are merely one component (O'RIORDAN & ZMUDA 2015; BLOWFIELD & MURRAY 2011). Subsequently, the term CSR has also been changed to CR when referring to publications in order to stay congruent, even though the term CSR was used in the publications. Skipping the word 'social' has no content-related consequence for the referred sources. The only exception is in chapter 2.2.1.3 where *Carroll's* 'CSR pyramid' is introduced and the formulation was not changed.

Furthermore, there are various related concepts such as corporate citizenship (MCINTOSH 2007), corporate sustainability (ELKINGTON 2007), and corporate social responsiveness (WOOD 2007), just to name a few, that are difficult to distinguish from each other and are used synonymously (CRANE ET AL. 2008). The wide variety of terms and concepts makes measuring and comparing studies and measurements difficult for theory and practice (DUONG DINH 2010). As explained previously, this work sticks consistently to the term CR that is described and defined in 2.2.1.

2.2.1 Conceptual history and definition of terms
2.2.1.1 Sustainability
The concept of sustainability began with respect to the natural environment and goes back to the preservation and conservation movements of the 18th and 19th centuries (CARROLL & BUCHHOLTZ 2015; VISSER 2007). The term 'sustainability' was first used in this context in 1987, in a report by the World Commission on Environment and Development chaired by Norwegian Prime Minister Gro Harlem Brundtland. The now world-renowned Brundtland report (WORLD COMMISSION ON ENVIRONMENT AND DEVELOPMENT 1987) coined what has become the most cited definition of sustainability and sustainable development:

»Sustainable development is development that fits the needs
of the present without jeopardizing the ability of future
generations to provide for their needs.«
(JONKER 2015, P. 28)

One decade later, *Elkington* broadened the concept of sustainability to economic and social considerations, the *triple bottom line* (TBL). The TBL forms the
basis for the concept of CR and suggests that managers balance the pursuit of
ecological and social goals while simultaneously achieving economic success
(ELKINGTON 1998):

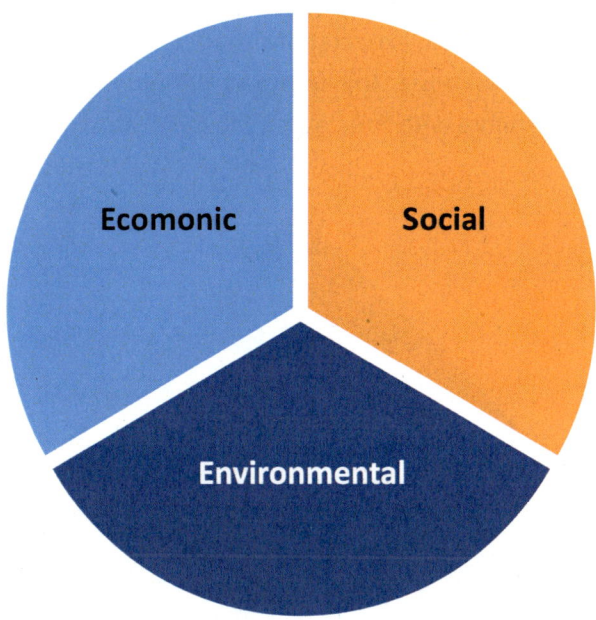

Figure 1: The three components of sustainability.
Source: Adapted from Elkington (1998).

A helpful means of linking CR with sustainability is this contemporary approach:
CR is not about how organisations spend their money but how they make it. This

means that companies integrate sustainability into their corporate strategy and business operations (O'RIORDAN, ZMUDA & HEINEMANN 2015).

In this context, *Visser's* unique interpretation of the commonly used acronym CSR (Corporate Social Responsibility) should be mentioned: It is 'Corporate Sustainability and Responsibility' (VISSER 2013).

2.2.1.2 CSR pyramid by Carroll

In 1979, *Carroll* provided the first popular definition of CSR, namely as a concept that refers to the general belief held by a growing number of citizens that modern businesses have responsibilities to society that extend beyond their obligations to the stockholders or investors in the firm (CARROLL 2007; VISSER 2011). In this regard, *Carroll* points out that CSR encompasses the economic, legal, ethical and discretionary or philanthropic expectations that society has at a given point in time (CARROLL & BUCHHOLTZ 2015). This four-part definition of CSR can be graphically depicted as a pyramid with four layers, the CSR pyramid:

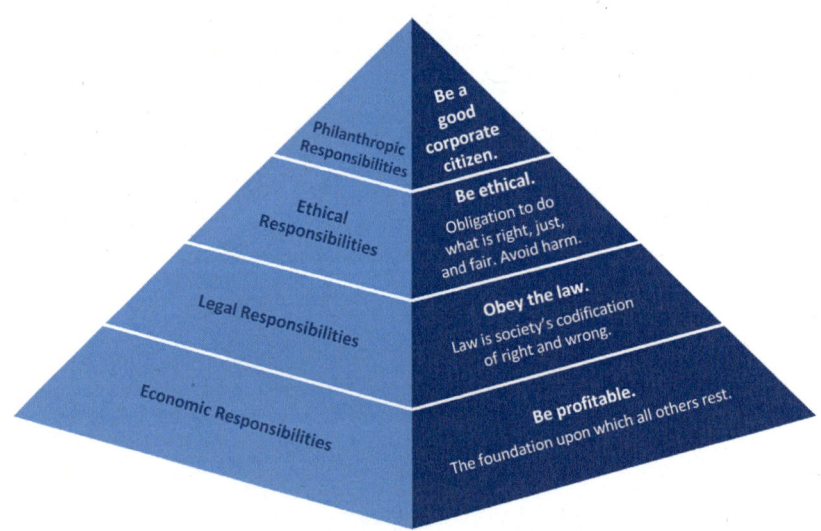

Figure 2: CSR pyramid.

Source: Adapted from Carroll & Buchholtz (2015).

The economic responsibility is the fundament of social responsibility, since corporations have first and foremost the responsibility to produce goods and services that society wants, to sell them at fair prices and to make profits in order to ensure their growth and to reward their investors. Since laws form the basis for the cooperation between society and the economy, business is expected to obey all laws. Ethical responsibilities embrace activities, standards, values and practices that are expected by society even though they are not formulated in laws. Therefore, ethical responsibilities are classified as voluntary, e.g. the philanthropic responsibility layer on top of the pyramid. This responsibility refers to every voluntary or discretionary activity for the benefit of society. The major distinction between ethical and philanthropic responsibilities is that the public does not expect the philanthropic ones (CARROLL & BUCHHOLTZ 2015). The CSR Pyramid was first published in 1991 and endures, together with *Carroll's* four-part definition, to this day (VISSER 2011). It is seen as the most established, accepted and fairly pragmatic model of CR (CRANE & MATTEN 2010). Nevertheless, there are also other opinions in contemporary literature stating that *Carroll's* approach from 1991 is outdated, old-fashioned and not included in any management concept (SCHNEIDER 2015).

2.2.1.3 Core characteristics of CR

It is impossible to provide a definitive answer as to what CR is or how it should be best realised. For a common understanding of how CR is generally interpreted and implemented these days, *Crane, Matten* and *Spence* suggest six core characteristics of CR. Few existing definitions will include all of them, but academic and practical definitions tend to reproduce them as essential features in some way. It is important to consider that the meaning and relevance of CR varies according to organisational and national background (CRANE, MATTEN & SPENCE 2008; CRANE, MATTEN & SPENCE 2014).

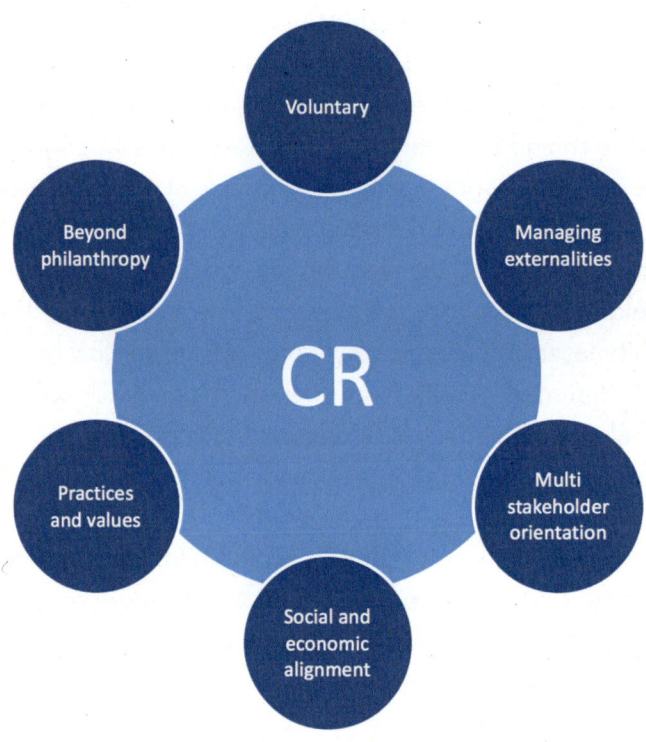

Figure 3: Core characteristics of CR.

Source: Adapted from Crane, Matten & Spence (2014).

Voluntary

CR is typically defined as a voluntary activity that goes beyond the law (IBID.).

Managing externalities

Externalities are the positive and negative side effects of economic behaviour that are not considered in a company's decision-making. They are also not included in the price of goods or services. Pollution is a typical example of an externality since society in general and local communities in particular have to cope with it. Legal regulations can force corporations to internalise the cost of the externalities but CR represents a voluntary approach to managing them. For example, investments in clean technologies, minimising carbon emissions, or managing human rights violations in the workforce (IBID.).

Multiple stakeholder orientation

CR implies considering various interests of several stakeholders[1] other than just the shareholders of the firm, because corporations have to interact with many parties such as consumers, employees and suppliers in order to survive and prosper (IBID.). Stakeholders are individuals or groups who have a 'stake', or vested interest, in the firm (BUCHHOLTZ & CARROLL 2012). The complexity of stakeholders in a company is shown in Figure 4:

Figure 4: Stakeholder map of a very large company.

Source: Adapted from Crane, Matten & Spence (2014).

1 For more detailed information on the stakeholder approach, please see 'Stakeholder Theory' by Freeman et al. (2010), which is a summary of discussions about the topic throughout three decades, beginning with Freeman's seminal work on the issue.

Social and economic alignment
Managing different stakeholder interests leads to another consideration. While CR may be about going beyond shareholder interests and profit-seeking, many people think CR should not conflict with profitability. On the other hand, CR is defined many times in the sense that aligning social and economic interests is a result of self-interest because firms can benefit economically from acting responsibly (CRANE, MATTEN & SPENCE 2014).

Practices and values
CR is about business practices that deal with social and environmental issues. But for many people CR is about more than that – it is a philosophical attitude, a set of values, a mindset that drives CR-related activities. This is one reason why CR is a highly discussed topic. It is not only about the actions of corporations, it is also about the motives for their actions (IBID.).

Beyond philanthropy
Philanthropy is an altruistic action designed to promote the good of society. In *Carroll's* CSR pyramid, philanthropy is the last step for which all the other more operational aspects of CR are a prerequisite (COHEN 2007). In some parts of the world, CR is mainly philanthropic; corporations support the less fortunate. Of late, the debate on CR has tended to lean more in towards the idea that CR is, in reality, much more than philanthropy, but refers to how a corporation as a whole impacts on society. A corporation, in this sense, refers to its core business functions. These are production, marketing, procurement, human resource management, logistics, finance, etc. This approach is based on the assumption that CR needs to be integrated into normal business practice rather than being a solely voluntary action (CRANE, MATTEN & SPENCE 2014).

2.2.1.4 CR in Germany
Since the research questions and objectives of this research focus on German consumers, it is also important to describe how CR is interpreted and implemented in Germany. The government of the Federal Republic of Germany issued a definition of CR (BUNDESMINISTERIUM FÜR ARBEIT UND SOZIALES 2016). Accordingly, CR includes social, ecological and economic aspects that are set out in internationally

accepted reference documents such as the ILO Tripartite Declaration on Multinational Enterprises and Social Policy (INTERNATIONALES ARBEITSAMT 2006), the OECD Guidelines for Multinational Enterprises (OECD 2011), the UN Guiding Principles on Business and Human Rights (DEUTSCHES GLOBAL COMPACT NETZWERK 2014), the UN Global Compact (GLOBAL COMPACT 2016) and the ISO 26000 standard (BUNDESMINIS-TERIUM FÜR ARBEIT UND SOZIALES 2011). In specific terms, CR includes issues such as fair business practices, employee-orientated personnel policies, the economic use of natural resources, the protection of the climate and environment, a serious commitment locally and responsibility in the supply chain.

Furthermore, it is stressed that CR activities vary from business to business and have to have a clear reference to the company's core business (BUNDESMINISTERI-UM FÜR ARBEIT UND SOZIALES 2016). This prerequisite corresponds to the earlier mentioned, contemporary approach to CR that CR is not about how organisations spend their money but how they make it.

Additionally, the government of the Federal Republic of Germany declared that from 2015 onwards, its CR strategy would be more internationally oriented (BUN-DESMINISTERIUM FÜR ARBEIT UND SOZIALES 2016A). At an international level, the European Commission's Communication on CR (EUROPÄISCHE KOMMISSION 2011) is decisive along with the UN Guiding Principles on Business and Human Rights (DEUTSCHES GLOBAL COMPACT NETZWERK 2014) and the OECD Guidelines for Multinational Enterprises (OECD 2011).

2.2.2 Design parameters for CR commitment

The CR activities of multinational companies affect millions of people all over the world through their products, their employees, the communities they locate in and the natural environment they harm. Hence, the matter of how corporations meet their responsibilities is an important one. Fundamentally, a corporation has responsibilities in four key arenas (CRANE, MATTEN & SPENCE 2014A):

1. CR in the marketplace
2. CR in the workplace
3. CR in the community
4. CR in the natural environment

With regard to the research questions and the research objectives of this work, only the first key arena, CR in the marketplace, is considered. Furthermore, the marketplace is divided into three different types of marketplace:

1. Consumer markets
2. Financial markets
3. Business-to-business markets

Since firms in the clothing industry focus mainly on end-consumers, only the consumer market is considered here. Some consumer markets such as the clothing industry gain a disproportionate amount of CR attention, because they directly affect the end-consumer and because activists and the media target them due to scandals such as those involving the labour conditions in the TCI (CRANE, MATTEN & SPENCE 2014).

The broad diversity of existing CR-definitions opens up a seemingly endless array of possibilities for CR practices. Corporate management chooses from the variety of options in order to achieve its corporate and sustainability goals (MÜNS-TERMANN 2007). There is no standard solution with respect to how firms should design and handle their CR activities (BUNDESMINISTERIUM FÜR ARBEIT UND SOZIALES 2016). Although many consumers express a commitment to rewarding responsible engagement, their actual market place behaviour does not always line up (CRANE, MATTEN & SPENCE 2014). Answers in surveys are susceptible to social desirability biases, where respondents give the answer they believe interviewers want to hear (BHATTACHARYA, SEN & KORSCHUN 2011). Moreover, there is significant heterogeneity across consumers in their reactions to CR activities; what works for one consumer segment does not automatically work for another (BHATTACHARYA & SEN 2004).

In view of all these considerations, one can derive a guiding principle for designing the parameters of CR commitment: the CR practices of a company and their extent depend on the company's goal and the company's stakeholders (MÜNSTER-MANN 2007).

2.2.3 Strategic use of CR commitment

According to the four-part definition of CR (economic, legal, ethical and philanthropic) by *Carroll* in section 2.2.1.2, the understanding of CR ranges from a more normative philosophy to an entrepreneurial flexibility. However, responsibility and profit are not seen as opposites these days. While, in the past, profitability and responsibility were long understood as distinct and competing (PORTER & KRAMER 2002), for *Drucker,* CR and profitability are not only compatible; CR can lead to economic success. According to *Drucker,* this means that it is the responsibility of a business to tame the dragon, i.e. to turn a social problem into an economic advantage, into productive capacity, into human competence, into well-paid jobs and into wealth (DRUCKER 1984). Consequently, there has been a trend termed 'strategic CR' since the 1980s. Strategic CR means that by investing in the responsibilities of the company, its competitiveness is strengthened (PORTER & KRAMER 2006). In a survey, Chief Executive Officers (CEOs) named reasons for their companies becoming more responsible. The top ten reasons included competitive advantage, cost savings and customer demands (SEN, DU & BHATTACHARYA 2009).

2.2.3.1 CR as a strategic management approach

The management consultancy firm PricewaterhouseCoopers defined CR as the systematic and long-term management of nonfinancial risks as well as opportunities. It defined the most important value drivers for integrated CR activities that lead companies to embed CR in their DNA (GASTINGER & GAGGL 2015):

Value drivers for integrated CR	
Minimizing risks	**Utilizing opportunities**
Securing reputational damages	Strengthening credibility and trust
Satisfaction of stakeholder's need for information and transparency	Brand loyalty through values and security
Safeguarding the future and quality assurance of products and services	Differentiation from competitors
Cost savings through energy and resource efficiency	Attracting/maintaining of qualified workforce
Security of supply (Versorgungssicherheit) regarding raw materials and energy	Innovation of products and services through sustainable concepts
Preparation for increasing regulation	Development of new market and customer segments
= Reduce costs	**= Increase market share**

Table 2: Important value drivers for integrated CR activities.

Source: Adapted from Gastinger & Gaggl (2015).

2.2.3.2 Profiling through CR commitment

At a time when consumers are discerning and the public is sensitised to social and ecological issues, CR is a profiling tool that engenders trust and acceptance (DUONG DINH 2010). Trust is an essential part of customer loyalty, as explained in section 2.3.1, and according to *Porter,* a business can differentiate itself from competitors in three ways: through the core product or service, through the price or through the customer relationship. Since companies in today's competitive environment consider differentiation in the first two factors to be difficult, corporations are focusing on strong customer relationships (LEVENS 2012). The issue of customer relationship management is defined in detail in section 2.3.

Furthermore, CR engagement strengthens a positive corporate reputation (IVEY 2007), which is described in paragraph 2.4. Corporations with CR activities also have a better corporate image (LUO & BHATTACHARYA 2006). The difference between reputation and image is discussed in section 2.4.1.

A good corporate image does influence the relationship between the company and its stakeholders. A good CR reputation not only fosters customer loyalty and customer confidence, it also leads to higher customer satisfaction. Additionally, CR activities have a positive impact on current and future employees. In the war for talent, CR initiatives play a strong supporting role, especially with the younger generation. CR activities humanise a company and lead also to higher motivation and satisfaction for existing employees (BHATTACHARYA, SEN & KORSCHUN 2008; LUO & BHATTACHARYA 2006; MAST & FIEDLER 2007; MAST 2013; SEN & BHATTACHARYA 2001). CR engagement lowers the level of employee turnover, maximises work effort and loyalty. The last-mentioned aspect, in particular, has huge implications: loyal customers make great brand ambassadors; employees who enjoy shopping where they work are likely to convey their personal enthusiasm to customers (BHATTACHA-RYA, SEN & KORSCHUN 2011).

CR engagement secures a corporation's licence to operate (DERESKY 2014). In the field of CR, the term generally refers to a company's social licence to operate, i.e. the acceptance of a corporation's impact on people, society and the environment by their stakeholders, or the public. Overall, CR activities can be a competitive advantage for a company (IVEY 2007A; MAST & FIEDLER 2007; PORTER & KRAMER 2006; RAUPP 2011).

2.2.3.3 Ethical consumption
Ethical consumption is the conscious and voluntary choice to opt for goods that are perceived to create a more preferable social, economic or environmental impact due to personal moral beliefs and values. Ethical consumption covers a range of activities such as boycotting certain companies because of poor social, ethical or environmental behaviour, buying fair trade or organic products, avoiding products made in sweatshops, etc. (CRANE & MATTEN 2010; SABAPATHY 2007).

The inevitable connection between consumption and social, economic and environmental impact has, in recent years, lead more and more people to consume ethically. According to regular research reports, more than twice as many people bought ethically produced products in 2013 than in 2009 (OTTO 2013). Other research points to consumers' increased likelihood of purchasing the products and services of companies that engage in CR activities. Respondents to a survey displayed a significantly greater intent to purchase from a company with a positive CR record than from one with a poor record (BHATTACHARYA, SEN & KORSCHUN 2011).

Since ethical consumption requires consumers with above average levels of income and high levels of education, ethical consumption is a phenomenon among well-off groups in post-industrialised countries (SABAPATHY 2007). In Germany, the so called 'Lohas' (supporters of lifestyles of health and sustainability) represent about 25 – 30 per cent of all consumers, and the trend is rising (VOGLER & GRASSER 2015). Therefore, for suppliers, ethical consumption is a reason to broaden their range of products in order to address an additional target group with high purchasing power.

However, it is important to mention at this point that research has shown that customers are not willing to pay more for 'sustainable' products or services despite knowing about the background and the long-term implications of the industry's current behaviour. The cheaper purchasing price is presently more important than the overall cost savings in the future and the ecological and social harm that only become visible in the future (HACKL 2015). Moreover, the concept of the 'ethical consumer' is a point of heated debate in the field of scientific research (DEVINNEY, AUGER & ECKHARDT 2010).

2.3 Customer Relationship Management

Strong and enduring stakeholder relationships are critical to a company's success, and customers, in particular, are one of the most important stakeholders in a corporation. Without the support of customers, such as through the demand for or purchase of goods and services, most organisations are unlikely to survive for very long (BHATTACHARYA, SEN & KORSCHUN 2011; CRANE & MATTEN 2010).

Customer Relationship Management (CRM) has become an important mantra in marketing; CRM is perhaps the most important concept of modern marketing (ARMSTRONG & KOTLER 2009; BUCHHOLTZ & CARROLL 2012). CRM describes the careful collection and handling of detailed customer information. CRM enables focused customer orientation to maximise customer loyalty, which in turn increases competitiveness (CHRISTOPHER, PAYNE & BALLANTYNE 2002; KOTLER ET AL. 2012; KOTLER, KEL-LER & BLIEMEL 2007; KOTLER, KELLER & OPRESNIK 2015).

2.3.1 Customer loyalty

Customer loyalty is one of the most important goals in the manufacturing and service industries; it costs five times more money to acquire a new customer than to retain an existing one (KOTLER & KELLER 2012; WITTKÖTTER & STEFFEN 2002). The importance of loyalty derives from its substantial impact on the company's long-term profit (SEN, DU & BHATTACHARYA 2009). Customer loyalty is a deeply held commitment to rebuy or re-patronise a product or service consistently in the future, despite situational influences and marketing efforts that could evoke switching behaviour (BHATTACHARYA, SEN & KORSCHUN 2011; KOTLER ET AL. 2012; OLIVER 1999; OLIVER 2010). According to *Oliver,* consumers go through four loyalty phases until they reach 'ultimate' loyalty:

1) Cognitive loyalty
In the first phase, loyalty is shallow in nature and directed toward the brand because of information such as price, features, etc. in comparison to alternative products or services (OLIVER 1999; OLIVER 2010).

2) Affective loyalty
The second phase of loyalty is a combination of cognition and affect. In affective loyalty, an emotional bond is established towards the brand with feelings such as sympathy or trust. Those emotions refer to the provider though, not its products or services. Research has proved that this stage of loyalty is still subject to the risk of switching. (BRUHN 2015; OLIVER 1999; OLIVER 2010).

3) Conative loyalty
In this stage of loyalty development, cognitive and affective loyalty is expressed through behavioural intention. Conation by definition implies a brand-specific commitment to repurchase. Conative loyalty is a state that involves the deeply held commitment to buy for the first time combined with a social commitment. Although the consumer has the intention to repurchase, this desire may be not realised, like any good intention (OLIVER 1999; OLIVER 2010).

4) Action loyalty

In the last phase, the intention from the previous stage is transformed into readiness to act, which is proved by corresponding figures regarding repeated purchases, recommendations, etc. The readiness to act is accompanied by a desire to overcome obstacles. For companies, this phase is extraordinarily important since all efforts at building up relationships with customers pay off for the first time (IBID.).

Loyalty phase	Phase characterised by ...	Result of the phase
COGNITIVE	Information	Positive net benefit
		Transaction specific satisfaction
AFFECTIVE	Emotions	Cumulative satisfaction
	Sympathy	Involvement
		Preference
		Emotional closeness / bond
		Cognitive consistency
CONATIVE	Psychological exchange costs	Attachment
		Cognitive consistency
ACTIONAL	Psychological and physical exchange costs	Factual repetition of behaviour

Table 3: Phases of loyalty.
Source: Adapted from Oliver (2010).

Although companies have established complex CRM systems to enhance relationships with customers, it appears that consumers cannot be bribed into loyalty. Empirical studies on the impact of relationship marketing programs that offer economic incentives for repeated purchases have reported either very small positive effects or even insignificant effects. Customers feel more manipulated than understood as a result. Because of the poor results of economic incentive-based loyalty programs, companies continue to search for effective ways to foster lasting, meaningful relationships with their customers (SEN, DU & BHATTACHARYA 2009).

2.3.2 Impacts of CR on customer loyalty

Such lasting, meaningful relationships with consumers can be generated through CR activities and demonstrated values of a company. Increasingly, people want information about a company's CR record to help decide which companies to buy from and work for (KOTLER ET AL. 2012). A study of frequent buyers of yogurts from a company with CR activities professes stronger loyalty to the brand than frequent buyers of yogurts from a company without CR activities. The same research shows that a positive CR record can help not only immediate sales, but also the intent of consumers to purchase into the foreseeable future (BHATTACHARYA, SEN & KORSCHUN 2011). Other research results confirmed that the CR activities of a company enhanced consumer loyalty (SEN, DU & BHATTACHARYA 2009).

Typically, such loyalty is an outcome of a consumer-company identification. This phenomenon is driven by individuals' need for self-identification and social identity that prompts them to develop a sense of attachment to chosen organisations. Such identification leads consumers to engage in behaviours favourable to the company, for instance loyalty and word of mouth recommendation. Since the awareness of ethical consumption and CR in general is rising constantly, as discussed in previous sections, another key condition for expressing loyalty is the consumer's personal support for the CR cause. If a company keeps supporting, what consumers believe in, they will keep coming back (BHATTACHARYA & SEN 2004).

2.4 Reputation

"Not even the best business
is worth a corporation's reputation."
(SCHULZ 2015, P. 330).

This statement by a financial institution says it all; intangible assets such as corporate reputation are growing in importance and are viewed as a company's most valued and competitive asset (GAINES-ROSS 2008). According to various research studies, reputational risk is among the top ten business risks and can damage even whole industries (PIWINGER 2014).

Since corporate reputation plays such an important role for companies, all systematic corporate activities for building, maintaining and repairing corporate reputation are subsumed under the term 'reputation management'. The existence of many reputational rankings shows the great importance of reputation and its effect on companies (EINWILLER 2014; FABER-WIENER 2015; MARTINS 2005).

The terms reputation and image are often used interchangeably in colloquial as well as in scientific usage (CHUN 2005; DAVIES 2011; HERGER 2006). Hence, both terms are defined in the next section.

2.4.1 Reputation versus image – definition of terms

According to research into definitions in the literature on marketing and communications, four different approaches to the interrelation between reputation and image exist (FLEISCHER 2015; HERGER 2006):

1) Reputation and image are the same
Authors who do not differentiate between the terms mostly use the term image and ignore the term reputation. This is a very superficial way of dealing with this issue.

2) Reputation differs from image
Authors with this opinion claim that the terms are based on different concepts and have nothing in common.

3) Reputation determines image
For authors with this view, image is an individual perception of reality. Opinions, attitudes, impressions and connotations from single persons regarding a subject are an image. Whereas reputation is a public perception that influences individual images.

4) Image determines reputation
According to this interpretation, reputation is a snapshot that includes different images. Therefore, an image is more stable and stronger than reputation.

Summarised, the literary discourse seems to tend toward the notion of two separate but similar constructs (EINWILLER, 2014; FLEISCHER 2015; HERGER 2006). The differentiation refers to the temporal stability and the corporate communications of the corporation. Corporate image is a rapidly changeable reflection that is built upon messages communicated by a company. On the contrary, reputation describes a more 'realistic' picture of a company, which is determined over many years by experiences and the communication of such experiences. Therefore, corporate reputation is a perceptual representation of a company's past actions and future prospects that describe the firm's overall appeal to all its key constituents. Reputation is a global, temporally stable judgement that is shared by both internal and external stakeholders (EBERL 2006; GOTTSCHALK 2011; MAST 2010). This work uses this conceptual distinction and definition. The term reputation is used preferentially.

2.4.2 Impacts of CR on reputation

Particularly as a consequence of the increasing number of corporate scandals since the 1990s, the discussion regarding the terms CR and reputation are interlinked in scientific discourse (EISENEGGER & SCHRANZ 2011; EISENEGGER & SCHRANZ 2011A; POTOCKI 2015). However, corporate reputation is one of the most common drivers for companies to address CR issues, because CR is a vital part of how a company is perceived (IVEY 2007). The most important pre-economic success factor regarding CR is establishing a good reputation (FABER-WIENER 2015).

There are various findings from surveys regarding the impact and consequences of CR on reputation: in a major survey of 199 companies in 30 countries, 97 per cent of the corporations believe that a good sustainability ranking has a positive effect on their corporate reputation (WEBER 2015). Another poll found that 80 per cent of CEOs believe that CR contributes to their company's reputation. That poll also found that the CEOs believe that reputational benefits can significantly increase their company's ability to recruit and retain employees. Additionally, reputational benefits appeal to and attract consumers, differentiate their corporation and its offerings in the market place, generate additional sales and achieve many other business benefits (MIRVIS 2011). Another consumer survey shows an improvement in a company's reputation through a perception of responsibility (SCHIEBEL 2015). Almost 15 per cent of a company's image is influenced by environmental protection, fair treatment of employees, and conservation of resources (HEINRICH & SCHMIDPETER 2013).

Obviously, a corporation's reputation and its improvement through CR initiatives is an important issue in the area of CR. Interestingly enough, reputation also makes a difference to the effects of CR practices. Companies with strong reputations will reap greater rewards from CR activities than those with poor reputations because stakeholders will carry goodwill into their evaluation of the CR. However, not only are stakeholders likely to be more aware of what companies with strong reputations are doing, they are also more likely to have a favourable bias to such regarding such companies' CR practices. That leads to a heightened sense of unity. On the other hand, companies with poor reputations or companies from industries that are perceived critically per se such as oil, tobacco or alcohol, often claim that the effect of CR activities is dampened because many stakeholders cannot get rid of the negative bias they already have (BHATTACHARYA, SEN & KORSCHUN 2011).

2.5 CR communication

As already mentioned in the introduction, a poll has revealed enormous ignorance amongst the German population regarding CR-active companies. This is suprising, considering the increased interest consumers are taking in CR activities which is a significant driver for CR communication (JAROLIMEK 2014). Additionally, CR activities have a huge impact on customer relationships and corporate reputation, and can be a competitive advantage (JAROLIMEK & RAUPP 2011), as already explained in paragraph 2.2.3.2. Therefore, CR plays an increasingly important role in communication (WESTERMANN & SCHMID 2012) – one in four TOP-500-companies in Germany has declared CR communication to be the most important field of activity within public relations (MAST 2013).

As described previously, it is in every corporation's interest to communicate its CR practises and make them public. Therefore, CR communication is an inherent and crucial part of CR (IHLEN, BARTLETT & MAY 2011; RAUPP, JAROLIMEK & SCHULTZ 2011). However, if, because of expected positive reactions, CR activities are announced but never realised, this is termed 'greenwashing'. Greenwashing also often exaggerates a corporation's good practices while downplaying or ignoring its harmful actions. When greenwashing is identified, it can lead to massive reputational damage and a wounded reputation is not easily or quickly repaired (ALSOP 2004; D'HEUR 2015; IVEY 2007B; RAUPP, JAROLIMEK & SCHULTZ 2011).

In the realm of CR, communication is no longer a one-way street – dialogical communication is needed to satisfy the customer's wish for transparency and participation (HUCK-SANDHU 2011; MAST 2013; STOCKI & LAPOT 2015; VISSER 2013).

2.5.1 CR communication instruments

There are plenty of communication tools available to present the CR activities of a corporation (HEINRICH 2013), but given the aforementioned consumer desire for transparency and participation, the internet affords unique opportunities such as dialogue, networking, time independence and globalism (PLEIL 2012). CR and social media are among the inevitable standards in terms of communication and corporate management (WAGNER & EICHHORN 2013). As a result, many companies have a special microsite for CR on their website. One consultancy firm for digital communications regularly examines the websites of 100 major German companies. 67 per cent of these companies have an extra microsite for CR as well as links to various social media-channels such as Facebook, Xing, Twitter and YouTube (HEINRICH 2013).

In the following, an overview of CR communication instruments is provided (IBID.):

Corporate Responsibility			
Media work	**Publications**	**Online**	**Events**
Dialogue with stakeholders	Putting focus on CR topics	CR on the internet	Framing CR topics
• Press mailing list – Journalist database • Press information • Professional articles / bylined features • Press photos • Press conferences • Press talks / Interviews • Visits at the editorial office • Basic press kit • Development of topics and agenda settings • Media monitoring and evaluation	• Sustainability report (integrated or standalone) • CR newsletter • CR topics in customer magazines • Company journal • CR topics in business reports • Image and info brochures • Bulletin board • Commercial, image and public relation advertisements	• Company or campaign website / landing page • Internet editorials • Online press portal • Social media • Intranet • Podcast / video	• Stakeholder dialogue: bilateral stakeholder dialogue, dialogue forum • Road shows • Events: expert talks, fairs, panel discussions, conferences • In-house trainings / staff workshops • Open house • Event calendar
CR campaigns			

Table 4: CR communication instruments. Source: Adapted from Heinrich (2013).

Effective communication of engagement is a critical part of CR (BHATTACHARYA, SEN & KORSCHUN 2011) since the achievement of CR communication goals depends on the right measures and their combination in order to reach the chosen target group (HEINRICH & SCHMIDPETER 2013). Generally, all stakeholders have the right to information about the CR activities of a company. According to a survey of communication experts from Germany, Austria and Switzerland[2], CR topics are mainly communicated through traditional channels such as the media/the press (25 per cent), internal communication (24.6 per cent), CR reporting (15.6 per cent), stakeholder-communication (13.6 per cent), blogs/social media (12.3 per cent), n.a. (6.4 per cent) and others (2.8 per cent) (HEINRICH 2013).

---

2 To obtain the original study, the author of this work contacted the Managing Director of Grayling, the PR agency that conducted the research. Unfortunately, the study is not available anymore. Therefore, the excerpts of the study that were included in the specified book (Heinrich 2013) are used.

The most CR-specific communication tool is CR reporting, also called sustainability reporting. Research shows that in 2011, 95 per cent of the 250 largest companies in the world were already issuing CR reports, up from about 35 per cent in 1999 (FIKA 2015). That proves that CR reporting has gone mainstream; there is no debate about reporting or not reporting sustainability anymore – the high rates of CR reporting in all regions proves it is now standard business practice worldwide (BHATTACHARYA, SEN & KORSCHUN 2011; KPMG 2013).

One reason for nonfinancial reporting is the increasing demand from various stakeholder groups and the general public for more comprehensive disclosure and transparency on the part of corporations (CRAWFORD & WILLIAMS 2011; HEINRICH 2013) on foot of numerous environmental catastrophes and growing concerns about corporations and their unscrupulous profit-seeking as already mentioned in section 2.2. Corporations themselves name reputational considerations as a key driver for CR reporting. Moreover, corporations are increasingly demonstrating that sustainability reporting provides financial value and drives innovation (KPMG 2011).

Nonfinancial reporting has its origins in the 1970s, when mainly western European companies published so called 'social balance sheets' with a focus on their social performance. In the 1980s, ecological aspects were added to the reports because of serious accidents such as the chemical catastrophe in Bophal, India in 1984, the nuclear catastrophe in Chernobyl in 1986, and the accident involving the oil tanker, the Exxon Valdez in Alaska in 1989. The reactive and justification-based nonfinancial reporting of the 1970s and 1980s turned in the 1990s into a proactive and competitive tool. More and more companies realised the competitive advantage of environmentally friendly behaviour as a result of consumers' stronger ecological consciousness. At the turn of the millennium, financial, social and ecological aspects were reported, separately from the compulsory annual report, with English terminology. Today, CR reports or sustainability reports increasingly contain *Elkington's* three components of sustainability: economic, social and environmental, as described in section 2.2.1.1. CR reports with only one or two of *Elkington's* three components rarely exist nowadays (FIFKA 2015).

Sustainability reporting is formally standardised. Although various standards for sustainability reporting do exist, the guidelines of the Global Reporting Initiative (GRI) are preferred worldwide (CLAUSEN & LOEW 2007; FIFKA 2015; HEINRICH 2013; JASCH 2015). In 1997, the GRI was established by the American environmental organisation Coalition for Environmentally Responsible Economics (CERES) and the United Nations Environment Programme (UNEP) (BURCKHARDT & HAMM 2013). 78 per cent of the largest 100 companies in 41 countries refer to the GRI reporting guidelines in their CR reports (KPMG 2013). In its latest version, the GRI 4.0 (GLOBAL REPORTING INITIATIVE 2016) contains 58 core indicators on social, environmental and economic issues - *Elkington's* three dimensions of sustainability.

Apart from a few countries such as Austria, CR reporting is generally voluntary thus far. That is going to change for the EU by the end of 2016. The European Commission issued a directive that makes CR reporting mandatory from the beginning of financial year 2017 (EUROPÄISCHE KOMMISSION 2016). Companies with more than 500 employees, of which there are approx. 6,000 companies in the EU, have to report on strategy, results and risks in six areas: environmental, social and employee-related matters, human rights, anti-corruption and bribery. Companies that are additionally listed on a stock exchange will also have to report on their diversity policy with regard to age, gender, geography, as well as the educational and professional background of their employees (FIFKA & LOZA ADAUI 2015; MÖLLER, KOEHLER & STUBENRAUCH 2015).

2.5.2 CR communication in trade

The retail sector has a particularly important and influential role in CR. Retailers shape the sustainability of their supply chains and determine the range of products and services available to consumers, therefore also their purchasing as well as their consumer behaviour (EGAN 2010; HACKL 2015).

Klaus Wiegandt, founder of the 'Stiftung Forum für Verantwortung' and former CEO of Metro AG, Germany's largest trading company, is of the opinion that sustainability, in other words the responsible management of the natural resources of our planet, will be the greatest challenge facing trade and society generally-speaking for the coming decades; and meeting the challenges associated with that is only possible, if society as a whole moves towards sustainable development (LUX 2012). To achieve this, communication is needed in two directions. Firstly, consumers need information about facts such as production chains or the 'ecological rucksack' of products and on how they need to change their consumer behaviour in order to contribute to climate protection (LUX 2013). Consumers also expect impeccable products that have done no harm and want to buy them from trustworthy companies that strive towards creating added value for all their stakeholders (SCHMIDPETER 2015).

Secondly, communication and interaction with manufacturers and suppliers are key. Besides a focus on costs, delivery reliability and product quality, retailers should ask about working conditions, the existence of sub-contractors and the establishment of standards throughout the supply chain. As a consequence of negative behaviour, retailers could take products out of the range, which is currently hard or even impossible to realise because of competition – the huge trading companies would need to cooperate (LUX 2013).

According to the survey in the previous paragraph regarding the importance of communication channels for CR activities, internal communication, which means the communication with employees within a company, is almost as important as external communication. This once again proves the strong effect of CR activities on employees. Especially in the retail sector, employees are particularly vital because many act as the 'face' of the company for the consumer (BHATTACHARYA, SEN & KORSCHUN 2011).

2.6 CR in the clothing industry

As already mentioned, CR is still a voluntary activity that goes beyond the law, and this is also true in the clothing industry. Sustainability standards are one aspect of CR that is particularly visible for consumers in the clothing industry; these are described in the next section. Furthermore, a Germany-specific, governmental initiative was founded in 2014, the Alliance for Sustainable Textiles (BÜNDNIS FÜR NACHHALTIGE TEXTILIEN 2016A), which is described in section 2.6.2. Additionally, companies in the garment industry run their own, independently selected CR activities; in the following, two examples are shown.

1) Worldwide enhancement of social quality by Tchibo
In order to enhance the working conditions at its 40 suppliers in Asia, Tchibo realised workshops conducted by external but local trainers for the managers of each clothing factory as well as nominated employees from the same factory (BERTELSMANN STIFTUNG 2015; BURCKHARDT 2013).

2) Starvation wages in sewing factories –
hessnatur performs pioneering work with study on wages
hessnatur has 142 suppliers in 32 countries and examined wages that fulfill the basic needs of the workers (IBID.).

2.6.1 Sustainability standards

The labelling of goods has its origins in the early history of humankind, as seen in early high cultures from Egypt to China. Beginning with seals on transported goods, the labelling of goods stood in early cultures primarily as a guarantee and to build confidence in the producer (LEITHERER 1994).

Modern-day labels, particularly those that reference norms and standards, continue to provide that guarantee and build confidence, not just for products but for services and processes too. Norms and standards are documents that specify requirements, lay down required characteristics and help to ensure the free movement of goods, thus encouraging exports. Standards promote efficiency and quality assurance in industry, technology, science and the public sector. Moreover, they serve to safeguard people and goods and to improve quality in all areas of life (DEUTSCHES INSTITUT FÜR NORMIERUNG 2016). Experts from the fields of industry, research, consumer protection and the public sector work together in standardisation organisations to develop market-oriented standards and specifications, such as the Deutsche Institut für Normierung e.V. (DIN), one of the world's leaders in standardisation. Standards deal with subjects ranging from A as in acoustics to Z as in zinc and are developed in a consensus-based process (DEUTSCHES INSTITUT FÜR NORMIERUNG 2016A; HARTLIEB, KIEHL & MÜLLER 2009). The terminology in the field of norms and standards is diverse: norm, normation, standardisation, standard, type, etc. are used synonymously or with different meanings, in scientific as well as in colloquial language (KLEINALTENKAMP 1993).

The definition of standard used in this work is clarified in the following. *Vries* extracted consistent features of standards from various definitions of standards from national and international standardisation organisations and derived a general, solution-orientated definition:

> *"Standardization is the activity of establishing and recording*
> *a limited set of solutions to actual or potential matching*
> *problems, directed at benefits for the party or parties involved,*
> *balancing their needs and intending and expecting that these*
> *solutions will be repeatedly or continuously used,*
> *during a certain period by a substantial number of the parties*
> *for whom they are meant."*
> (VRIES 2010, P. 13).

Hansen and *Krull* define sustainability standards or their visualisation through eco-labels in that labels as product identifications guarantee certain ecological or social standards (HANSEN & KRULL 1994). Sustainability standards help people to consume ethically and therefore promote responsible economic consumer behaviour (BUNDESMINISTERIUM FÜR WIRTSCHAFTLICHE ZUSAMMENARBEIT UND ENTWICKLUNG 2016A). The process of labelling includes evaluation, information aggregation, and marking of certain statements of fact for the information of market participants. An eco-label is the final result of a multi-stage process through which the eco-label as a condensed, ecology-related overall judgement obtains its significance. An eco-label can consist of a word, a mark or a combination of both (HANSEN & KRULL 1994). According to *Kersten*, eco-labels can only exist, when a standard exists (KERSTEN 2012) and has been complied with (BUNDESMINISTERIUM FÜR VERKEHR UND TECHNOLOGIE 2009). In this work, the term label is used, when visualisation for market participants is meant.

Sustainability standards for clothing or rather for parts of the clothing chain can be organised into three groups (BUNDESMINISTERIUM FÜR VERKEHR UND TECHNOLOGIE 2009):

1) Human ecological criteria:

Textile auxiliaries used in the production chain are tested as to whether they are allergenic, carcinogenic, or hormonally effective.

2) Environmental criteria:

Effects of the production process on the environment are examined. If, e.g., cotton is cultivated biologically, without pesticides and fertilisers, or if wool comes from controlled biological livestock.

3) Social criteria:

Working conditions such as child labour, regulated working hours or minimum wages are controlled.

The compliance with standards and norms can be certified. The word certification derives from Latin 'certe' which means sure, certain and 'facesso' which means prepare, do, make (STOWASSER 1960). A certification is defined through five characteristics:

As

1) an official, written assessment (certificate)

2) by an impartial third party

3) that a certain object

4) fulfils certain requirements

5) that were set by an independent body (BRUHN 2013).

In Germany, the term 'eco' is not protected for clothing, though it is for organic food (HOLDINGHAUSEN 2015). Subsequently, there is a huge number of eco-labels for clothing, including company-independent ones and companies' own ones. In Appendix 4, a selection of company-independent eco-labels is described that are also part of the online survey.

2.6.2 Alliance for Sustainable Textiles

In 2014, German Federal Minister for Economic Cooperation and Development Gerd Müller established the Alliance for Sustainable Textiles (BÜNDNIS FÜR NACH-HALTIGE TEXTILIEN 2016A). The alliance is voluntary with the goal of achieving social, ecological and economic improvements throughout the production chain in the clothing industry. By May 2016, over 180 alliance partners from the worlds of business, NGOs, trade unions and the German Federal Government had joined (BÜNDNIS FÜR NACHHALTIGE TEXTILIEN 2016). Alliance partners include companies such as H&M, C&A, KiK, Tchibo, ALDI and LIDL (BUNDESMINISTERIUM FÜR WIRTSCHAFTLICHE ENTWICKLUNG UND ZUSAMMENARBEIT 2016). These huge multinational companies sell a great deal of clothing since they are discounters or retailers of fast fashion.

In June 2016, the Alliance for Sustainable Textiles complied with the 'Manufacturing Restricted Substances List' (MRSL) (ZDHC 2015). Consequently, all of the over 180 alliance partners undertook to replace more than 160 problematic chemicals with harmless alternative materials; further regulations with regard to improved working conditions are about to be completed (BÜNDNIS FÜR NACHHALTIGE TEXTILIEN 2016B). The MRSL and thereby the Alliance for Sustainable Textiles and its members are going beyond the legal stipulations of the European chemicals regulation 'Registration, Evaluation, Authorisation and Restriction of Chemicals (REACH)' (UMWELTBUNDESAMT 2016). Since the MRSL is internationally known and is not restricted to Europe, one also has the opportunity to achieve improvements in production. Another declared aim of the Alliance for Sustainable Textiles is to avoid excessive overtime hours and improve living wages (IBID.).

2.7 Results of the literature review

The literature review performed provides background information on the TCI and verifies the serious consequences of this industry and its production conditions. Furthermore, the concept of CR and its importance for business become clear. These aspects, together with the long-term significance of CR and its current status in the garment industry, are also explained. Since a search of official sources identified that no data is accessible regarding German consumers and their preferred socially responsible and sustainable fashion labels, the main aim of this research study, i.e. to answer the three research questions, was not possible yet. The three research questions still are:

1) What criteria determine socially responsible and sustainable behaviour according to German consumers' perceptions of fashion labels?

2) Which fashion labels are perceived as socially responsible and sustainable by the German consumer?

3) Through which communication measures do clothing companies achieve a socially responsible and sustainable perception?

3 METHODOLOGY

To answer these research questions, a qualitative research design approach (THEO-BALD & NEUNDORFER 2010) is undertaken. To this end, primary data are used. Firstly, an online survey is conducted, which is a quantitative method within the qualitative research design. To get an overall impression of the situation with regard to CR in the clothing industry throughout Germany, 504 women are interviewed. Secondly, the empirical data of the online survey are validated via qualitative interviews, with what are called 'expert interviews' (FLICK 2014). This approach is called triangulation (DIEKMANN 2005; FLICK 2014).

All documents used in this research including the online survey, its results and evaluations as well as the expert interviews and fact sheets of the eco-labels from the survey can be found in the appendix.

3.1 Triangulation

Triangulation in qualitative research contains different perspectives on the research objective and on the answers to the research questions. Those different perspectives could be variously applied methods or different theoretical approaches. The reason for triangulation is to increase knowledge (FLICK 2008; FLICK 2011); the aim of triangulation is never to reach a complete agreement between the results of the different methods, it is more about comparing the results (MAYRING 2002) in order to increase knowledge (FLICK 2011).

In this research, the findings of the online survey are triangulated with expert interviews which is called data triangulation (FLICK 2008).

3.2 Online survey

To answer the research questions, the author chose an online survey using a panel (KUTSCH 2007; GÖRITZ 2003). Such panels, also called access-pools (WELKER, WERNER & SCHOLZ 2005), collect potential respondents who have signed up to an organisation which provides people for market research surveys (POYNTER 2010). The members of an online access panel get an incentive to participate in online surveys (GÖRITZ 2003). Panels are the main reason why online quantitative research has become the leading data collection modality worldwide (POYNTER 2010). The use of online access panels has various advantages (THEOBALD 2014):

- Reliability of the data because of high willingness and motivation to participate
- Robustness of the sample through verified socio-demographic data
- Precise determination of the responses
- No distortions of the sample
- Geographically wide variety
- No interviewer effects

On the other hand, there are various limitations of a panel (KUTSCH 2007; HAUPTMANNS & LANDER 2003):

- No representativity of the collected data for the overall population
- No interviewer plus self administration makes the survey less controllable, e.g. interferences, many interviewees
- Insincerity because of anonymity

3.2.1 Online access panel provider

In order to ensure 500 responses to the online survey, the service provider respondi AG (RESPONDI 2016) conducted the online survey. The company continually develops survey methods and interview techniques in cooperation with the Survey Design and Methodology departement at the German Leibniz Institute for Social Sciences (GESIS 2016). respondi maintains its own actively managed online access panels. For the technical side of operations, the company uses a powerful software solution to manage its panels. With a combination of various online and offline recruitment methods, the panels reflect samples. respondi recruits the members of these panels via its own campaigns (RESPONDI 2016A).

3.2.2 Statistical population

The statistical population of the online survey is 504 women throughout Germany between the ages of 15 and 49. The size of the age groups in the survey is proportional to the size of the age groups in the total population of Germany:

Age Group	Number	Share
15-19	46	9%
20-29	141	28%
30-39	141	28%
40-49	176	35%
Sum	504	100%

Table 5: Statistical population of the online survey.
Source: Own illustration.

The reason for asking only women is that women are, on average, more interested in clothing, spend more money on fashion and shop more frequently than men (SPIEGEL 2015; SPIEGEL 2015A). The age span 15 to 49 is chosen because German people of that age have the greatest buying power, at 53 per cent (GFK 2010).

The panel is compiled with regard to the population density of each Federal State of Germany in proportion to the total population of Germany.

The basic population of women between 15 and 49 living in Germany is about 17.4 million (DESTATIS 2016). The larger the sample size, the more accurate the results of the survey. How well the sample represents a population is mainly defined by two values, which are the margin of error and the confidence level (SUE & RITTER 2012). The confidence level indicates the long-run probability that the results are correct, i.e. it determines the likelihood that the result of the sample is the same result as from any other randomly picked sample (ZIKMUND ET AL. 2013). A confidence level of 95 per cent is commonly used.

The margin of error describes the range in which the results of the sample can differ from the results of the basic population. In this case, a margin of five per cent has been chosen which means the results of the population would differ between plus or minus five percentage points from the results of the sample. Based on the population size, the confidence level and the margin of error the sample size should be 385. As panel providers usually offer packages with certain sample sizes, a size of 504 has been chosen which lowers the margin of error to about 4.4 per cent. This explanation does not mean that this online survey is representative though. In practice, the survey had 504 responses. 1,598 women were invited to participate, which means the response rate was 32 per cent.

3.2.3 Questionnaire

The author of this work designed the questions for the online survey questionnaire herself. The questionnaire consists of ten content-related questions. There are three questions at the beginning of the survey with regard to socio-demographic data such as age, gender and federal state. These questions ensure that only people, who belong to the defined statistical population, participate. If one answer to the three socio-demographic questions does not fit, the survey ends automatically.

The ten content-related questions are closed-ended, open-ended (FAULBAUM, PRÜFER & REXROTH 2009) and questions with response scales, so called 'Likert-scales' (DIEKMANN 2005; KIRCHHOFF ET AL. 2010). On the basis of Likert-scales, the extent of agreement or rejection is evident (IBID.).

In the questionnaire, open-ended questions always appear once again as closed-ended questions in order to help the participants if they cannot answer the question right away.

Generally, the questions are formulated to be as short and simple as possible. Moreover, the questions are formulated to be as neutral as possible (ATTESLANDER 2010; GLÄSER & LAUDEL 2010). Although the questions are written to be as neutral as possible, some of them touch on areas of social desirability and are therefore delicate questions (WOLTER 2012). Delicate questions are questions that provide the possibility of internal or external threat if answered truthfully. Furthermore, questions are delicate if there is a threat of disclosing socially undesirable behaviours or attitudes. Social desirability can lead to response bias, which means the interviewee does not tell the truth if it is not socially acceptable (IBID.). This phenomenon is also called the attitude-behaviour gap and describes a lack of validity within research (DEVINNEY, AUGER & ECKHARDT 2010).

The questions of the online survey and the expert interviews do not answer the research questions on their own. The author of this work and questionnaire-designer did this intentionally, because the chosen questions should create a more comprehensive, overall picture of the research topic allowing an outlook and providing indications for further research.

3.3 Expert interviews
Expert interviews are guided interviews (GLÄSER & LAUDEL 2010; MAYRING 2002) with people who normally have occupational expertise in a subject area; those people are usually employees in specific positions within companies (FLICK 2014). In in-depth interviews with various experts in the field of CR or the clothing industry, the results of the online survey have been triangulated. The problem-focused interviews (FLICK 2014; MAYRING 2002) were carried out via telephone, because all interviewees are busy executives with tight schedules. Therefore, it was not possible to interview the experts face-to-face. The author of this work designed the questionnaire for the expert interviews herself. Like the online survey questionnaire, the questions for the expert interviews are formulated to be as short, sim-

ple and neutral as possible (ATTESLANDER 2010; GLÄSER & LAUDEL 2010).
The following experts have been interviewed:

1) Hilke Anna Patzwall
MANAGER SUSTAINABILITY & CSR, 'VAUDE'
(SUSTAINABLE FUNCTIONAL CLOTHING FOR SPORTS AND LEISURE)

2) Anne Fries
PARTNER, 'CONCERN GMBH'
(CONSULTANCY FOR CR MANAGEMENT)

3) Mark Starmanns
CO-FOUNDER, 'GET CHANGED! THE FAIR FASHION NETWORK'
(ONLINE PLATFORM FOR SUSTAINABLE FASHION)

4) Claudia Kersten
DIRECTOR MARKETING & FINANCE AND REPRESENTATIVE
FOR GERMANY, AUSTRIA, SWITZERLAND, 'GOTS'
(GLOBAL ORGANIC TEXTILE STANDARD - SUSTAINABILITY STANDARD)

5) Peter Blunck
FOUNDER AND CEO, 'BAND OF RASCALS'
(ORGANIC BOYS CLOTHING)

6) Sven Bergmann
EXPERT CORPORATE COMMUNICATIONS, 'HESSNATUR'
(SUSTAINABLE FASHION)

7) Wolfgang Grupp
OWNER, 'TRIGEMA'
(SPORTSWEAR AND CASUAL FASHION)

The interviewer explained at the beginning of each interview that CR in this interview refers to the ecological, economic and social dimension.

3.4 Evaluation of the online survey and the expert interviews

The service provider respondi AG delivered the results of the online survey in two electronic documents; in an SPSS-document, which is a software program for statistics, and in an Excel-document, which is a software program for spreadsheet analysis. The author of this work evaluated and interpreted the results of the online survey as well as the expert interviews herself. To evaluate the answers to the survey, the author formed categories in which the various answers were classified (FLICK 2014). To evaluate the open-ended questions four and nine, the respective answers were analysed. Based on the analysis, answer categories were created and afterwards the answers given were associated to one or more of these categories. Answers that could not be assigned to one category were summed up under 'Others'. For question four, in particular, the categories are not distinct due to the vague nature of the answers. Participants often answered 'no exploitation', which can be congruent with 'fair wages' or 'good working conditions' or both.

To evaluate the expert interviews, a content-related structuring (DIEKMANN 2005; GLÄSER & LAUDEL 2010) was chosen. According to *Mayring,* structuring is the most important content-analytically technique (MAYRING 2003).

For example, with regard to question three, the average ranking for CR issues was calculated by weighting the individual rankings of the experts; rank one received three points, rank two received two points, rank three received one point and no rank received zero points. Then, the sum of the weighted ranks was divided by the number of experts. The resulting numbers were arranged in descending order to get the overall ranking across all individual expert rankings.

4 RESEARCH FINDINGS

4.1 Results of the online survey

The first three questions of the online survey are socio-demographic questions in order to ensure that only people of the defined statistical population participate.

Question four, the first content-related, open-ended question after the socio-demographic ones, asks the participants about their understanding of the CR of companies in the clothing industry. More than one third of the survey participants, 33 per cent, could not answer the question. This is why the same question was asked once again with response options in order to help the participants by suggesting answers. The five most frequently given answers to the open-ended question and the five most frequently given answers to the closed-ended question correspond with each other:

Question 4/5: What does CR of companies in the clothing industry mean to you?					
Open-ended question 4, Multiple answers possible			Closed-ended question 5, Multiple answers possible		
Question answered: 339 women (67%) Question not answered: 165 women (33%)			Question answered: 504 women (100%)		
Response category	Men-tions	Share*	Share*	Men-tions	Response category
Fair wages (no cheap labour, social benefits)	142	42%	89%	450	No child labour
Good working conditions (fair treatment, appreciation, work safety)	117	35%	88%	441	Fair wages
Environmentally friendly production, sustainability	102	30%	87%	438	Good working conditions
No child labour	83	24%	78%	391	Environmentally friendly production (dyeing, bleaching, processing, etc.)
No chemicals / toxins in clothes	37	11%	75%	377	Non-toxic clothes

*Share of women who answered the question, i.e. named at least one reason.

Table 6: Results of question 4/5. Source: Own illustration.

The three most often mentioned answers to question four, the open-ended version, are fair wages, good working conditions and environmentally friendly, sustainable production. In the closed-ended question five, these three aspects ranked second, third and fourth place. The aspect 'No child labour', the most frequently selected answer to the closed-ended question five, is in fourth position in the open-ended version. The fifth most often mentioned answer to open-ended question four is 'No chemicals/toxins in clothes', which is also the fifth most frequently mentioned answer to question five. In summary, for the German consumer fair payment, good working conditions, no child labour and environmentally friendly production as well as non-toxic substances are the most important criteria for CR with regard to fashion labels.

Question six asks about the importance of the CR of companies when purchasing clothing. 86 per cent or 432 women answer very important or important, whereas 14 per cent or 72 women answer rather unimportant or unimportant. With regard to the age groups, there is no major departure within each answer option. That means 20 per cent of the 15-19-year-old, 22 per cent of the 20-29-year-old, 22 per cent of the 30-39-year-old, and 26 per cent of the 40-49-year-old women find CR very important. 65 per cent of the 15-19-year-old, 65 per cent of the 20-29-year-old, 62 per cent of the 30-39-year-old, and 60 per cent of the 40-49-year-old find CR important. 13 per cent of the 15-19-year-old, 12 per cent of the 20-29-year-old, 14 per cent of the 30-39-year-old, and 13 per cent of the 40-49-year-old find CR rather unimportant. Finally, two per cent of the 15-19-year-old, 1 per cent of the 20-29-year-old, 1 per cent of the 30-39-year-old, and 2 per cent of the 40-49-year-old find CR unimportant.

Question 6, closed-ended: How important is the CR of companies in the clothing industry to you when purchasing clothing?										
	Total		Age 15-19		Age 20-29		Age 30-39		Age 40-49	
	Men-tions	Share	Men-tions	Share	Men-tions	Share	Men-tions	Share	Men-tions	Share
Very important	116	23%	9	20%	31	22%	31	22%	45	26%
Important	316	63%	30	65%	92	65%	88	62%	106	60%
Rather unimportant	65	13%	6	13%	17	12%	20	14%	22	13%
Unimportant	7	1%	1	2%	1	1%	2	1%	3	2%
Sum	504	100%	46	100%	141	100%	141	100%	176	100%

Table 7: Results of question 6. Source: Own illustration.

The next question, question seven, asks about three fashion labels, which are known as being active with regard to CR. Initially, the question is formulated as an open-ended one. 69 per cent of the statistical population, i.e. 347 women, did not answer the question. 157 women or 30 per cent answered the question. Three answers are invalid, because the answers did not make sense, e.g. '...' or 'I do not know'.

Compared to the closed-ended version of the same question, question eight, more than one third of the statistical population, 194 women or 38 per cent, did not make any entry, which is still more than one third of the statistical population. The 15 most frequently picked fashion labels from a given list are:

Question 7/8: Which three fashion labels do you know as being active with regard to CR?					
Open-ended question 7			Closed-ended question 8		
Question answered: 157 women (31%) Question not answered: 347 women (69%)			Question answered: 310 (62%) Question not answered: 194 women (38%)		
Brand	Men-tions	Share*	Share*	Men-tions	Brand
H&M	29	18%	26%	80	hessnatur
Esprit	26	17%	20%	62	C&A
C&A	19	12%	19%	60	H&M
Trigema	13	8%	19%	58	Tchibo
S.Oliver	13	8%	18%	56	Esprit
Armed Angels	12	8%	16%	49	Trigema
Adidas	10	6%	14%	43	Adidas
hessnatur	10	6%	11%	35	Lidl
Nike	9	6%	10%	32	Benetton
Puma	7	4%	10%	30	S. Oliver
Tom Tailor	6	4%	9%	29	Vaude
Tchibo	4	3%	9%	27	Nike
Lidl	4	3%	8%	25	Armed Angels
Zara	4	3%	6%	20	Puma
Kik / fairtrade / Desigual Bio / Vero Moda	3	2%	6%	20	Aldi

*Share of women who answered the question, i.e. named at least one brand.

Table 8: Results of question 7/8. Source: Own illustration.

All of the five most often named fashion labels from question seven, the open-ended question, are also among the ten most often named fashion labels from question eight, the closed-ended version. The most often named fashion labels from question eight are placed sixth, seventh, eighth, ninth and tenth on the list from question seven of the 15 most frequently named fashion labels.

Two sustainable fashion labels, Armed Angels and hessnatur, are placed sixth and eighth in the answers to the open-ended question seven.

When considering the age groups in the closed-ended question eight, see the figure below listing the 15 most frequently cited brands, one can see that the frequency with which C&A is mentioned is very similar across all age groups. The fashion labels, for which mentions in both rankings do not vary more than three positions, are C&A, H&M, Esprit, Trigema, Adidas and Nike.

Question 8, closed-ended: **Which three fashion labels do you know as being active with regard to CR?**										
	Rank		15-19 years		20-29 years		30-39 years		40-49 years	
Brand	Closed-ended	Open-ended	Men-tions	Share*	Men-tions	Share*	Men-tions	Share*	Men-tions	Share*	Total Nom.
hessnatur	1	8	4	11%	28	33%	24	30%	24	22%	80
C&A	2	3	7	20%	18	21%	17	21%	20	19%	62
H&M	3	1	7	20%	12	14%	17	21%	24	22%	60
Tchibo	4	13	7	20%	18	21%	10	12%	23	21%	58
Esprit	5	2	7	20%	13	15%	18	22%	18	17%	56
Trigema	6	4	4	11%	11	13%	15	19%	19	18%	49
Adidas	7	7	9	26%	7	8%	9	11%	18	17%	43
Lidl	8	14	3	9%	10	12%	9	11%	13	12%	35
Benetton	9	X	2	6%	10	12%	11	14%	9	8%	32
S.Oliver	10	5	6	17%	8	9%	5	6%	11	10%	30
Vaude	11	17	2	6%	10	12%	12	15%	5	5%	29
Nike	12	9	6	17%	7	8%	7	9%	7	6%	27
Armed Angels	13	6	2	6%	10	12%	11	14%	2	2%	25
Puma	14	10	3	9%	4	5%	4	5%	9	8%	20
Aldi	15	X	3	9%	6	7%	2	2%	9	8%	20

Share of women who answered the question, i.e. named at least one brand.

Table 9: Results of question 8 by age groups. Source: Own illustration.

Question nine is an open-ended question and asks why the previously named fashion labels are known as being committed to CR. The ten most often cited brands from question eight are evaluated, multiple answers are permitted. When summing up the named reasons across all ten fashion labels and ranking them afterwards, the top three reasons for knowing about the CR commitment are:

1) Sustainable/environmentally friendly production/offering sustainable products
2) Conveyed through advertising
3) Found out from the media (read/seen/heard)

Question 9, open-ended: How did you learn about the CR activities of the previously named fashion labels?		
	Mentions*	**Share***
Sustainable / environmentally friendly production / offering sustainable products	92	18%
Conveyed through advertising	88	17%
Found out from media (read / seen / heard)	61	12%
Have good working conditions	32	6%
Word-of-mouth advertising (by family, friends, other contacts)	30	6%
Produced in Germany	28	6%
Provide good quality / good value-for-money ratio	28	6%
Products have eco seal or label	25	5%
No child labour	14	3%
Paying fair wages	14	3%
Support fair trade	8	2%
Recycle old clothes	6	1%
Are socially committed	5	1%
Protect animal rights	4	1%
Others	64	13%
Do not know / no reason	84	17%

*Total mentions of this reason across all ten brands.

**Share of the total mentions across all reasons and all ten brands.

Table 10: Results of question 9. Source: Own illustration.

The most often cited reason by 26 women with regard to the label hessnatur is 'Sustainable/environmentally friendly production/offering sustainable products', which with 18 votes is the top reason for C&A too, and for Tchibo with twelve mentions. The most often cited reason with 27 votes or 55 per cent for fashion label Trigema is 'produced in Germany' and the second most often named reason is 'pay fair wages' with ten votes. Eight women answered 'eco-labels' for C&A as well as six women for H&M.

Question ten is a closed-ended question and asks how the respondents learnt of the CR activities of the previously named fashion labels. The participants are able to select one or more channels from a predefined list. The mentions per channel are summed up and the share of the total amount of mentions is calculated. The three most frequently mentioned reasons for the perception of the label as being active in CR are:

1) The shop with 30 per cent of all mentioned channels, 216 mentions, or 15 times being among the three most often named ways.

2) The channel website with 24 per cent of all mentioned channels, 171 mentions, or twelve times being among the three most often named ways.

3) The channel TV with 23 per cent of all mentioned channels, 169 mentions and 13 times being among the three most often named channels.

Question 10, closed-ended: How did you learn about the CR activities of the previously named fashion labels?		
	Mentions*	Share*
Shop	216	30%
Website	171	24%
TV	169	23%
Family/Friends	150	21%
Newspaper/Magazine	140	19%
Social Media	125	17%
Outdoor advertising	71	10%
Others	51	7%
Direct mail advertising	50	7%
Flyer	35	5%
Radio	15	2%

*Total mentions of this channel across all brands.

**Share of the total mentions across all channels and brands.

Table 11: Results of question 10. Source: Own illustration.

The following mentions are striking:

C&A, with 33 votes and 53 per cent, has the most mentions of all labels for the top channel shop, followed by H&M with 28 votes or 47 per cent for the channelshop, and Tchibo with 27 votes or 47 per cent. hessnatur, the winner of closed-ended question eight, has 23 mentions or 29 per cent for the second-placed channel website. With regard to the third top channel TV, the label Trigema has by far the most votes with 33 or 67 per cent.

If one looks at the preferred channels of each age group, it is remarkable that the winning channel shop is ranked first in each of the four age groups, relatively balanced with 22, 18, 19 and 19 per cent respectively. The internet, with social media or website, is ranked second or third for the 15-19-year-old and 20-29-year-

old women. For the two older age groups, the relevance of online channels decreases. Instead, the channel TV is more important for them and is third for both
groups. This entire spreadsheet is very complex and is included in the appendix.

Question eleven provides a Likert scale for the answer and asks about the importance of eco-labels when purchasing clothing. 44 per cent or 221 women answered very important or important, whereas 56 per cent or 283 women answered
rather unimportant or unimportant.

Question 11, closed-ended: How important are eco-labels for you when purchasing clothes?		
	Mentions	**Share**
Very important	39	8%
Important	182	36%
Rather unimportant	236	47%
Unimportant	47	9%
Sum	504	100%

Table 12: Results of question 11.

Source: Own illustration.

Question twelve is an open-ended question and asks about known eco-labels for
clothing, multiple answers are permitted. 388 women or 77 per cent said they did
not know an eco-label for clothing, whereas 116 women knew one or more eco-
labels. By far the most mentions, with 39 are for the label Fairtrade, which garner-
ed 34 per cent of the votes. Oeko-Tex received far fewer with 13 votes or eleven
per cent and in third place is Blauer Engel with nine mentions.

Question 12/13: Which eco-labels for clothing do you know?					
Open-ended question 12			**Closed-ended question 13**		
Question answered: 116 women (23%) Question not answered: 388 women (77%)			Question answered: 504 women (100%)		
Brand	**Men-tions**	**Share***	**Share***	**Men-tions**	**Brand**
Fairtrade	29	34%	80%	403	Textiles Vertrauen nach Oeko-Tex Standard 100
Oeko-Tex	13	11%	72%	363	Blauer Engel
Blauer Engel	9	8%	70%	354	Fairtrade Certified Cotton
Bio	9	8%	11%	55	GOTS
Bio Baumwolle	8	7%	7%	36	Keine
Bio Cotton	7	6%	6%	31	Cradle to Cradle
Textiles Vertrauen	7	6%	4%	19	Internationaler Verband der Naturtextilwirtschaft
GOTS	7	6%	1%	3	Others

*Share of women answering the question, i.e. naming at least one eco-label.

Table 13: Results of question 12/13. Source: Own illustration.

The last question of the online survey is question 13, the same question as question twelve, but closed-ended. Multiple answers are also permitted. Textiles Vertrauen/Oeko-Tex Standard placed first with 403 votes or 80 per cent. Then comes Blauer Engel with 363 votes or 70 per cent, closely followed by Fairtrade Certified Cotton with 354 mentions or 70 per cent. The top three answers for both questions correspond, but in different order.

4.2 Results of the expert interviews
Question one asks the experts how important, in their opinion, CR for fashion labels is for the public. Three experts are of the opinion that the importance of CR is increasing. Two experts think that CR is important. One expert feels it is very

important for many people and one believes it to be unimportant for the overall population.

The next question, question two, deals with the development of the importance to consumers of CR for fashion labels. All the experts agree that the importance is increasing, but they differ in how they see the extent of the increase. Three experts describe the importance of this issue as increasing 'rapidly', 'definitely' and 'absolutely', with another two describing the increase as 'doubtless' and 'very clear'. However, two others think that the increase is not significant. One expert says the importance 'is tending to increase' and one expert says that 'one has to look for the increase in importance of CR', which means, that the increase in his opinion is low.

To answer question three, the experts had to name the most important aspect of CR of fashion labels for the consumers. As described at the beginning of chapter four, the order of the named aspects is weighted. The weighted average looks as follows: Working conditions are ranked first, the second most important aspect for consumers is the environment or environmental protection, while no chemicals or harmful substances are in third place.

Question 3: What is the most important aspect of CR of fashion labels for the consumers?	Rank Expert 1	Rank Expert 2	Rank Expert 3	Rank Expert 4	Rank Expert 5	Rank Expert 6	Rank Expert 7	Ave-rage*	Total rank
Working conditions	3	2	1	3	2	1	1	2.1	1
Environment	1	0	2	2	0	1	2	1.7	2
Chemicals / toxics	2	1	0	1	1	0	0	1.6	3
Social fairness	0	0	1	0	0	0	1	0.9	4
Consumer protection	2	0	0	0	0	0	0	0.3	5

*Average of weighted ranking.

Table 14: Results of the expert interview, question 3. Source: Own illustration.

Question four asks the experts which gender they assume to be more interested in and informed about the CR of fashion labels. Four experts reckon that there is no difference between male and female. One expert believes that women are more interested and two experts are convinced that women are more interested in the CR of fashion labels.

Question five deals with the connection between age groups and the importance of CR. The opinions of the experts are diverse. Two experts think that people of all ages are interested in the topic of the CR of clothing manufacturers. One expert reckons that people aged 18-55 years consider the issue important, whereby the older they are the tendency is to be more interested. One expert holds the opposite view: the importance of CR decreases from 45 years onwards and young people are more conscious about the topic. One expert thinks that young parents and grandparents are very interested in the topic. Another expert also assumes that the importance of CR comes with parenthood, maturity and sufficient financial resources, i.e. parents plus 30-year-old people onwards. One expert assumes that the importance of the topic comes with maturity, which begins with the mid/end 20s and is linked to the life experience of older people.

Question six deals with the target group for CR in the fashion industry. The experts were asked to define their target groups/the target group for CR in the fashion industry. Three experts agree on this that the target group is people of all ages. One expert defines the target group for his products as parents of boys from one to approx. eleven years old. Another expert defines the target group of the company she works for as 18-55-year olds. One expert assumes the target group consists of people about 30-35-years old and older and the seventh expert defines the main target group of the company he works for as women in their mid-40s and older, better educated, very interested and discerning.

Question seven asks about the knowledge of eco-labels. The opinions are mixed again. Four experts think the knowledge is predominantly bad or very bad, another expert thinks this knowledge is increasing. One expert finds that eco-labels are definitely known and one expert is of the opinion that the knowledge depends on the social background of the people. Three experts mentioned the vast array of eco-labels as an additional difficulty for the consumer.

To answer question eight, the interviewees had to estimate the relevance of eco-labels for the purchase of clothing. One expert refers to the customers of his company, and for them eco-labels are unimportant. Two experts are finding that their relevance is increasing, one expert thinks they are of low importance and another two experts say if clothing is fashionable, an eco-label can be the decisive purchase argument. One expert mentions that eco-labels are a help to consumers, which is contradicted by the large variety of existing labels.

Question nine asks about appropriate communication channels for reaching people interested in fashion labels that are engaged in CR. Six out of seven experts mention online channels such as online shops and blogs; one of these experts refines this by saying that young people, in particular, are reachable through social media and another one says 99 per cent of their clothing is sold online. Another expert mentions only the point of sale (POS) and the online shop. The only expert, who does not mention online channels explicitly thinks that fairs for sustainable products are a very good platform for reaching such people, that TV is too uncertain and specific channels for organic food or organic cosmetics are also suitable. Other than that, three experts emphasise the POS as an extraordinarily important channel, one of them also mentions the catalogue as equally important for their customers as the POS.

Question ten, the last question in the expert interviews, deals with the future of CR in the clothing industry and what the experts predict. One expert says the future of CR in the garment industry depends on the overall economic development, because CR is generally dependent on economic trends and that a circular economy is going to become a trend. The other six experts are sure of the ongoing development and increasing importance of CR in the clothing industry. Two of them mention in this context the licence to operate, which CR is going to become, and another two experts refer to the German Alliance for Sustainable Textiles, which is described in section 2.6.2.

5 Discussion

The results of questions four and five of the online survey and the third question of the expert interviews answer the first research question of this work, which is "What criteria determine socially responsible and sustainable behaviour according to German consumers' perceptions of fashion labels". The corresponding result of the survey and the expert interviews are as follows:

1) Good working conditions (such as fair wages, no child-labour, no exploitation, fair treatment, appreciation, work safety, social benefits, etc.)
2) Environment and environmental protection
3) Absence of chemicals and harmful substances in the clothing

This result is very interesting in so far as one might think the most important aspect for consumers is their own health with regard to chemicals and harmful substances in clothing, as experts two, four and five expressed in the interviews. Interestingly enough, however, the survey as well as the expert interviews show that people have a strong altruistic interest in their fellow human beings and the environment.

The CR of fashion labels is obviously important for consumers when buying clothing. Question six from the survey says that 86 per cent of the women surveyed considered CR to be very important or important when buying clothing. This is confirmed by another study (NIELSEN 2015) which reveals the readiness of customers to pay more money for products from companies that are active in CR. In 2015, 52 per cent of German people were prepared to spend more money for such products, which is an increase of 20 per cent in comparison to 2011, when 32 per cent of all Germans claimed that. Of course, one has to take into account possible response bias because of social desirability, as explained in section 3.2.3, but the experts also highlight this situation and the trend with their stated opinions in question one of the expert interviews.

The fact that, according to question seven of the survey, 69 per cent of the women surveyed do not know a fashion label that is active in CR, supports the poll cited in section 1.1 that 82 per cent of the German population does not know a company that stands for environmental and climate protection while taking social concerns into account. In the closed-ended version, more than one third of the women did not make an entry either. One interpretation of the results suggests that the communication of CR activities by companies is not good enough. A second important point is that two of the leading brands given in the answers to the survey, H&M and C&A, have for several years ranked amongst the most popular clothing labels in Germany (VUMA 2015). It is possible that both brands are named automatically because of their popularity.

The most frequently named clothing label in the closed-ended question eight is hessnatur. The fact that the word nature is part of the brand name could tempt people to choose the brand. On the other hand, Armed Angels, the other clothing label with a business model based on CR and sustainability, reached position six in the open-ended question seven, even though the brand name does not reference its focus on CR and sustainability.

The answers to open-ended question nine provide information on how consumers know about the CR-activities of the previously named brands. The two most popular answers 'Found out from the media (read/seen/heard)' and 'Conveyed through advertising' prove that the question was not well-formulated by the author of this work. The answers should provide information about the activity of the clothing company that lead to the perception. Instead of asking 'How do you know about the CR commitment of the previously named fashion labels?' a better question would have been: 'Through which CR-related activity are the three previously named fashion labels known to you as being committed to CR?' The answers would have provided even more information about the significance of CR in the clothing industry, and would have served as a means of double-checking survey-questions four and five. However, the answers given do prove the particular importance of appropriate CR communication by companies as described in paragraph 2.5.

Concerning the closed-ended question ten of the survey and the most often chosen channels, hessnatur as the most often cited CR-committed fashion label, has 23 mentions or 29 per cent for the channel website. This corresponds to the statement by expert six, an expert in corporate communications at hessnatur, that since 2013 hessnatur has sold more clothing online than via catalogue or POS. On the website, it states '40 Jahre hessnatur – 40 Jahre nachhaltig & fair' ('40 years of hessnatur – 40 years of sustainability & fairness') with a hyperlink to a microsite that tells the whole story and background of hessnatur and its focus on sustainability.

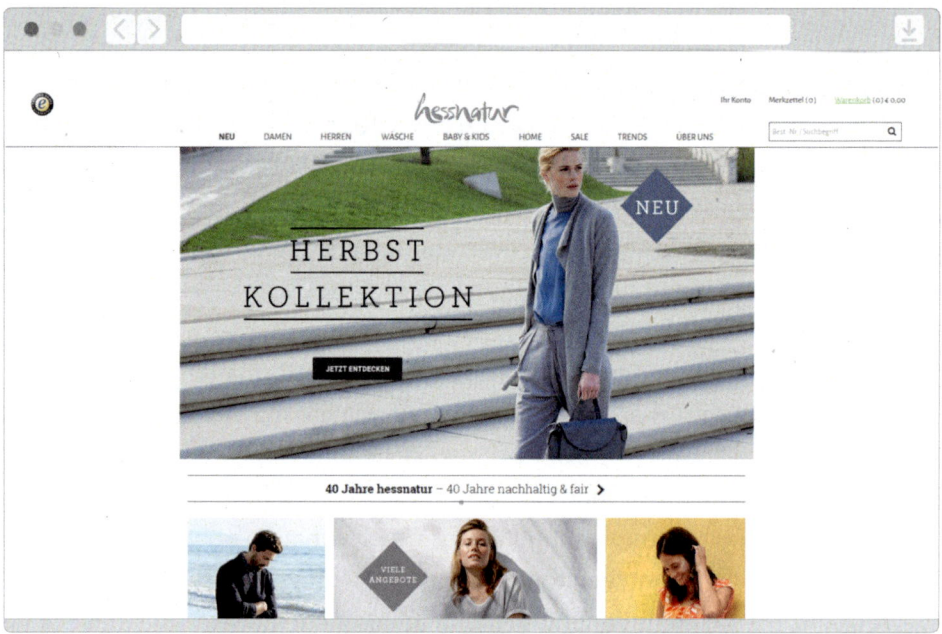

Figure 5: Landing page hessnatur. Source: hessnatur (2016).

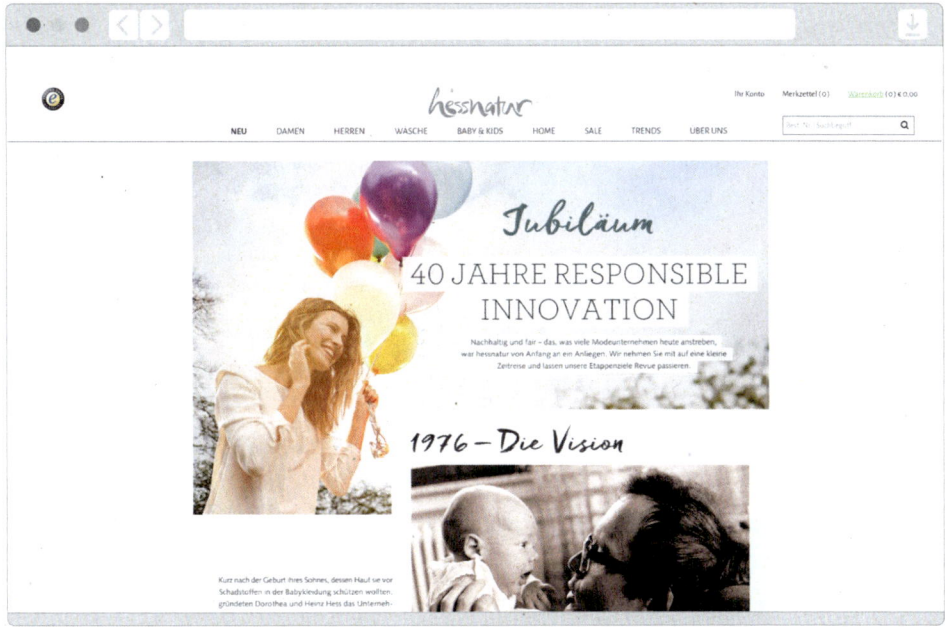

Figure 6: Microsite with history of hessnatur. Source: hessnatur (2016a).

Since the channel 'shop' is the winner of all channels and within this channel, there are three winners, C&A with 33 votes, H&M with 28 and Tchibo with 27, the author of this paper visited the stores of the three brands. In a C&A store, there were large 'Bio Cotton' sign on the sales floor (SEE FIGURE 7 AND 8).

Figure 7: C&A-store, Schildergasse, Cologne. Source: Own photograph.

Figure 8: C&A-store, Schildergasse, Cologne. Source: Own photograph.

In a H&M store, there were signs stating 'Basics aus Bio-Baumwolle' ('basics made of organic cotton') on the sales floor (SEE FIGURE 9) and 'Nachhaltigere Mode und sauberes Wasser' ('more sustainable fashion and clean drinking water') over the cash desk (SEE FIGURE 10). Moreover, in the store there are recycling containers where customers can recycle their old clothes (SEE FIGURE 11).

Figure 9: H&M-store, Schildergasse, Cologne. Source: Own photograph.

Figure 10: H&M-store, Schildergasse, Cologne. Source: Own photograph.

Figure 11: H&M-store, Schildergasse, Cologne.

Source: Own photograph.

In the Tchibo-store, there is product packaging with the statement '100 Prozent Bio-Baumwolle' ('100 per cent organic-cotton') (SEE FIGURE 12) or 'Cotton made in Africa' (SEE FIGURE 13), which is an eco-label. Other than that, there is no sign or hint regarding CR or sustainable production in the store.

Figure 12: Tchibo-store, Rheincenter, Cologne. Source: Own photograph.

Figure 13: Tchibo-store, Rheincenter, Cologne. Source: Own photograph.

With regard to the third top channel TV, Trigema has by far the most votes of all fashion labels with 33 mentions or 67 per cent. On watching TV-advertisements for Trigema on YouTube, several results of the survey become clear. It is said in the advertisements that Trigema produces solely in Germany and that the owner of Trigema assumes responsibility for his employees and the natural environment. These three aspects deemed most important by the participants of this survey as well as by the experts, when it comes to corporate responsibility of clothing companies; this advertisement on TV is obviously the reason for several results of the survey. Firstly, Trigema is in fourth position in open-ended question seven, the three CR-active clothing companies. Secondly, in open-ended survey-question nine, the reason for knowing that the previously mentioned fashion labels are active in CR, 27 women or 55 per cent mentioned 'produced in Germany', which is the highest result of all ten fashion labels in this category. These results underline the importance of the channel TV in communication.

Since none of the experts mentions TV as an important channel and one expert is uncertain of its importance, the medium TV is obviously underestimated by the experts.

Figure 14: TV-advertisement by Trigema. Source: Trigema (2012).

It is striking that three experts talk about where the products are sold in their answers, despite being asked about appropriate communication channels. That leads to the assumption that they confused sales channel and communication channel.

The result of question eleven is that 44 per cent of the women find eco-labels to be very important or important, whereas 56 per cent find them rather unimportant or unimportant. This means, more than half of the women of each group find them unimportant, rather unimportant or that their importance is increasing. This corresponds with the results of the expert interviews. In a nutshell, two experts say labels are unimportant and not very important, two experts believe that their relevance is increasing, two experts consider labels an add-on and one expert finds them generally helpful but too complex. Surprisingly, only 113 women voted for eco-labels in closed-ended question five, despite 221 women saying in question eleven that eco-labels are very important or important to them. This leads to the assumption that social desirability has distorted the results of question eleven.

The suspicion of response bias because of social desirability in question eleven seems to be confirmed when the results of question twelve are considered. 388 women say they do not know an eco-label. In question eleven, only 183 women said eco-labels are rather unimportant or unimportant to them. That is a gap of more than 200 women. One should be able to name at least one eco-label, when one considers them important or very important.

However, the result of closed-ended question five, where 113 women say eco-labels represent the CR of clothing companies to them, is confirmed by question twelve where 116 women name at least one eco-label; the difference is only three women. The reason for that could be that these three women remember an eco-label having seen the word/picture symbol, which is understandable. One survey discovered that two thirds of interviewed German recipients recognised the eco-label Oeko-Tex Standard 100 by its logo (IFH 2012). The clear winner of question twelve is Fairtrade, even though this label is not specifically for clothing, as shown in its factsheet in the appendix. This could be the reason for its top ranking in the open-ended question twelve, because Fairtrade has been present and visible on the market for many years in many segments, such as coffee and chocolate. The picture below shows a billboard in a Tchibo-store with the Fairtrade-logo. Tchibo originally became popular for selling coffee (SEE FIGURE 14).

Figure 15: Tchibo-store, Rheincenter, Cologne. Source: Own photograph.

The eco-label Oeko-Tex Standard 100 is the winner in question 13, which is closed-ended; Blauer Engel and Fairtrade certified cotton are in second and third place respectively. The survey mentioned in the last paragraph came to the same result with regard to the Oeko-Tex Standard 100; this eco-label is well-known in Germany. According to an international survey, the eco-label Oeko-Tex Standard 100 is actually the best-known eco-label for clothing worldwide (IFH 2012).

6 CONCLUSIONS

The first research question 'What criteria determine socially responsible and sustainable behaviour according to German consumers' perceptions of fashion labels?' is answered by questions four and five of the online survey and question three of the expert interview. The three most important criteria are firstly good working conditions, secondly environmentally friendly production and thirdly an absence of chemicals or harmful substances in clothing. As already mentioned, there is consensus between the results of both the survey and the interviews.

The second research question 'Which fashion labels are perceived as socially responsible and sustainable by the German consumer?' is answered by questions seven and eight of the online survey. The top five fashion labels that are perceived as socially responsible and sustainable by the consumers are hessnatur, C&A, H&M, Tchibo, and Esprit. However, the fact that in the open-ended question seven, 69 per cent of the women asked could not name a single label that is active in CR and in the closed-ended question eight still 38 per cent of the women did not perceive any of the listed labels as committed to CR is a clear sign that CR communication needs to be improved. This result confirms the poll cited in section 1.1, according to which 82 per cent of the German population does not know a CR-committed company.

The third research question 'Through which communication measures do clothing companies achieve a socially responsible and sustainable perception?' is answered by survey-question ten and expert interview-question nine. The most often mentioned answer in the survey is shop in first position in all age groups, then website in second position, closely followed by TV in third position. Social media plays a larger role for younger women, while TV is more important for older women. The results of the expert-interview do not correspond completely, but are generally in line. Since the medium TV comes very close after the medium website in the results of the survey and the experts do not consider TV as an important channel at all, this is a clear deviation in the research results. The results of the survey largely comply with the results of the literature review in section 2.5.1; the medium POS is not considered at all in the literature but plays, according to the online survey, a crucial role. As experienced and photographed in the shops of selected fashion labels, the companies are aware of that. Although eco-labels are a fixed part of the clothing industry, the survey and the expert interviews reveal that eco-labels currently do not play a very important role in communicating CR activities.

With respect to the limitations of the research approach used for this master's thesis, several aspects have to be pointed out:

1) Social desirability leads to a response bias, as described in the literature review and evidenced in the survey; see section five, survey-question six.
2) Since the respondents of the online survey are paid to take part, their commitment towards answering open-ended questions is not very high, meaning the answers to the open-ended questions are not many and often not detailed. This contradicts the stated advantages of online access panels found in the literature review in section 3.2, where it says, the willingness and motivation of the participants is high.
3) A questionnaire without an interviewer in an online survey limits the information one can get, if a question is not formulated precisely enough, as for example survey-question nine. There is no chance of correcting or digging deeper. Therefore, pre-testing of questionnaires is highly recommended.

7 OUTLOOK

This study suggests that deeper investigation is required into the field of ethical consumption and the personal attitudes of consumers. The altruistic intention revealed by research question one could intimate a response bias because of social desirability, but the fact that the experts are of the same opinion would contradict that. Increasing turnover figures for ethically produced products also contradict a response bias. On the other hand, research has proven that consumers are unwilling to pay more for sustainable products. These conflicting findings call for further research.

Since CR is still voluntary and corporations, in particular, have such a huge impact and thus huge power, the Alliance for Sustainable Clothing has the potential to initiate real change. The experts interviewed for this study predicted, almost una-nimously, a strong development in the clothing industry in the coming years; two of them independently mentioned the Alliance for Sustainable Clothing, another two called CR 'a license to operate in the future'. Such predictions are supported by the reporting obligation for specific corporations which is to take effect from the beginning of 2017 onwards. Will the reporting obligation impact on business practices?

Another possible avenue of study arising from this thesis would be to verify if the perceived CR-activities of the clothing companies are actually taking place and to interview the companies about them.

Moreover, in this work, only women have been interviewed, because they spend more money on fashion and shop more frequently than men. It would be very interesting to interview men and compare the results.

Despite a much-heightened awareness of the negative consequences of the ma-nufacturing processes in the clothing industry both for people and the environ-ment, there is still a long way to go to rectify the damage; it is even questionable whether the environment can ever recover from this damage.

The textile and clothing industry is one of the largest in the world, and has a huge impact on the global economy, environment and people. Its practices and condi-tions, and the consequences they have for us all, are not only worthy for further investigation, they demand it.

References

ALSOP, R. (2004). *The 18 Immutable Laws of Corporate Reputation.*
New York: Wall Street Journal Books.

ARMSTRONG, G. & KOTLER, P. (2009). *Marketing.* New Jersey: Pearson Prentice Hall.

ATTESLANDER, P. (2010). *Methoden der empirischen Sozialforschung.* Berlin: Erich Schmidt.

AUST, C. (2015). *Meine Kinder sind gerade ein ökologischer Albtraum.*
[http://www.faz.net/aktuell/stil/mode-design/andrew-morgan-ueber-seinen-
film-the-true-cost-13609237.Html] Accessed 26 May 2016.

BERTELSMANN STIFTUNG (2015). *CRI Corporate Responsibility Index 2015.*
[http://www.cr-index.de/downloads/Gesamtbericht_CRI_2015.pdf]
Accessed 10 August 2016.

BHATTACHARYA, C. & SEN, S. (2004). *Doing better at doing good:*
When, why, and how consumers respond to corporate social initiatives.
[http://www.davideacrowther.com/csrmodule/csrreading4b.pdf]
Accessed 07 August 2016.

BHATTACHARYA, C., SEN, S. & KORSCHUN, D. (2008). Using corporate social responsibility to
win the war for talents. *MIT Sloan Management Review,* (49)2, 37-44.

BHATTACHARYA, C., SEN, S. & KORSCHUN, D. (2011). *Leveraging Corporate Responsibility.*
New York: Cambridge University Press.

BECKERT, S. (2014). *King Cotton.* München: C.H. Beck.

BLOWFIELD, M. & MURRAY, A. (2011). *Corporate Responsibility.*
New York: Oxford University Press.

BRUHN, M. (2013). *Qualitätsmanagement für Dienstleistungen.* Heidelberg: Springer Gabler.

BRUHN, M. (2015). *Relationship Marketing*. München: Vahlen.

BUCHHOLTZ, A. & CARROLL A. (2012). *Business & Society: Ethics and Stakeholder Management*. Canada: Cengage Learning.

BUND, BROT FÜR DIE WELT & EVANGELISCHER ENTWICKLUNGSDIENST (2009). *Zukunftsfähiges Deutschland in einer globalisierten Welt*. Frankfurt am Main: Fischer.

BUNDESMINISTERIUM FÜR ARBEIT UND SOZIALES (2011). *Die DIN ISO 26000 "Leitfaden zur gesellschaftlichen Verantwortung von Organisationen"*. [http://www.bmas.de/SharedDocs/Downloads/DE/PDF-Publikationen/a395-csr-din-26000.pdf?__blob=publicationFile] Accessed 03 June 2016.

BUNDESMINISTERIUM FÜR ARBEIT UND SOZIALES (2016). *Nachhaltigkeit und CSR*. [http://www.csr-in-deutschland.de/DE/Was-ist-CSR/Grundlagen/Nachhaltigkeit-und-CSR/ nachhaltigkeit-und-csr.html] Accessed 03 June 2016.

BUNDESMINISTERIUM FÜR ARBEIT UND SOZIALES (2016A). *CSR in der EU*. [http://www.csr-in-deutschland.de/DE/Politik/CSR-international/CSR-in-der-EU/csr-politik-der-eu.Html] Accessed 03 June 2016.

BUNDESMINISTERIUM FÜR VERKEHR UND TECHNOLOGIE (2009). *Ökotextil-Labels in Österreich*. [http://images.umweltberatung.at/htm/oekotextillabels_in_oesterreich.pdf] Accessed 24 June 2016.

BUNDESMINISTERIUM FÜR WIRTSCHAFT UND ENERGIE (2016). *Textil und Bekleidung*. [http://www.bmwi.de/DE/Themen/Wirtschaft/branchenfokus,did=196528.html] Accessed on 20 May 2016.

BUNDESMINISTERIUM FÜR WIRTSCHAFTLICHE ZUSAMMENARBEIT UND ENTWICKLUNG (2015). *Bündnis für nachhaltige Textilien*. [https://www.textilbuendnis.com/images/pdf/Publikationen/BMZ_Das_Buendnis_f%C3%BCr_nachhaltige_Textilien_August_2015.pdf] Accessed 03 June 2016.

BUNDESMINISTERIUM FÜR WIRTSCHAFTLICHE ZUSAMMENARBEIT UND ENTWICKLUNG (2016). *Beitrittswelle zum Textilbündnis – führende Unternehmen erklären Mitgliedschaft.* [http://www.bmz.de/de/presse/aktuelleMeldungen/2015/juni/20150602_Beitritts welle-zum-Textilbuendnis-fuehrende-Unternehmen-erklaeren-Mitgliedschaft /index.html] Accessed 03 June 2016.

BUNDESMINISTERIUM FÜR WIRTSCHAFTLICHE ZUSAMMENARBEIT UND ENTWICKLUNG (2016A). *Mehr erfahren über Umwelt- und Sozialsiegel.* [https://www.siegelklarheit.de/ bewertung/#a1] Accessed 06 June 2016.

BURCKHARDT, G. (2013). *Corporate Social Responsibility – Mythen und Maßnahmen.* Wiesbaden: Springer Gabler.

BURCKHARDT, G. (2014). *Todschick.* München: Random House.

BURCKHARDT, G. & HAMM, B. (2013). Nachhaltigkeitsberichterstattung auf Grundlage der Global Reporting Initiative. In G. Burckhardt (Ed.): *Corporate Social Responsibility – Mythen und Maßnahmen,* (pp. 197-201). Wiesbaden: Springer Gabler.

BÜNDNIS FÜR NACHHALTIGE TEXTILIEN (2016). *Factsheet: Bündnis für nachhaltige Textilien* [https://www.textilbuendnis.com/images/pdf/Factsheet/160628_ Factsheet_B%C3%BCndnis_f%C3%BCr_nachhaltige_Textilien.pdf] Accessed 12 May 2016.

BÜNDNIS FÜR NACHHALTIGE TEXTILIEN (2016A). *Bündnis für nachhaltige Textilien: Über uns.* [https://www.textilbuendnis.com/de/startseite/das-textil-buendnis] Accessed 03 June 2016.

BÜNDNIS FÜR NACHHALTIGE TEXTILIEN (2016B). *Bündnis für nachhaltige Textilien strebt Mode ohne Gift an.* [https://www.textilbuendnis.com/images/pdf/Presse_de/2016-06-28_PM_Buend nisfuernachhaltigeTextilien_ZDHC_18072016.pdf] Accessed 25 July 2016.

CARROLL, A. (2007). Corporate Social Responsibility. In W. Visser, D. Matten, M. Pohl, & N. Tolhurst (Eds.): *The A to Z of Corporate Social Responsibility*, (pp. 122-131). West Sussex: John Wiley & Sons.

CARROLL, A. & BUCHHOLTZ, A. (2015). *Business & Society: Ethics, Sustainability, and Stakeholder Management.* Stamford: Cengage Learning.

CHRISTOPHER, M., PAYNE, A. & BALLANTYNE, D. (2002). *Relationship Marketing.* Oxford: Butterworth-Heinemann.

CHUN, ROSA (2005). Corporate reputation: Meaning and measurement. *International Journal of Management Reviews*, 7(4), 91-109.

CLAUSEN, J. & LOEW, T. (2007). Leitlinien und Standards der Nachhaltigkeitsberichterstattung. In G. Michelsen & J. Godemann: *Handbuch Nachhaltigkeitskommunikation*, (pp. 614-622). München: oekom.

CLEAN CLOTHES CAMPAIGN (2012). *Deadly Denim.* [http://www.cleanclothes.org/ resources /publications/ccc-deadly-denim.pdf] Accessed 18 May 2016.

CLEAN CLOTHES CAMPAIGN (2014). *Im Stich gelassen: Die Armutslöhne der Arbeiterinnen in Kleiderfabriken in Osteuropa und der Türkei.* [http://lohnzumleben.de /wp-content/uploads/2014/06/CCC-GE-ExSum-GER-DEF-LR-spreads1.pdf] Accessed 18 May 2016.

COHEN, J. (2007). Philanthropy. In W. Visser, D. Matten, M. Pohl & N. Tolhurst (Eds.): *The A to Z of Corporate Social Responsibility*, (pp. 363-365). West Sussex: John Wiley & Sons.

CRANE, A. & MATTEN, D. (2010). *Business Ethics.* New York: Oxford University Press.

CRANE, A., MATTEN D. & SPENCE, L. (2008). Corporate social responsibility: in a global context. In A. Crane, D. Matten & L. Spence (Eds.), *Corporate Social Responsibility* (pp. 3-20). Oxon: Routledge.

CRANE, A., MATTEN D., & SPENCE, L. (2014). Corporate social responsibility: in a global context. In A. Crane, D. Matten, & L. Spence (Eds.), *Corporate Social Responsibility* (pp. 3-26). Oxon: Routledge.

CRANE, A., MATTEN D. & SPENCE, L. (2014A). CSR in the marketplace. In A. Crane, D. Matten, & L. Spence (Eds.), *Corporate social responsibility: in a global context.* (pp. 213-251). Oxon: Routledge.

CRANE, A., MCWILLIAMS, A., MATTEN, D., MOON, J., SIEGEL, D. (2008). The Corporate Social Responsibility Agenda. In A. Crane, A. Williams, D. Matten, J. Moon & D. Siegel (Eds.), *The Oxford Handbook of Corporate Social Responsibility* (pp. 3-15). Oxford: Oxford University Press.

CRAWFORD, E. & WILLIAMS, C. (2011). Communicating Corporate Social Responsibility through Nonfinancial Reports. In O. Ihlen, J. Bartlett, S. May (Eds.), *The Handbook of Communication and Corporate Social Responsibility,* (p. 338-357). West Sussex John Wiley & Sons.

DAVIES, G. (2011). The meaning and measurement of corporate reputation. In R. Burke, G. Martin & C. Cooper (Eds.), *Corporate Reputation* (pp. 45-60). Surrey: Gower Publishing Limited.

DERESKY, H. (2014). *International Management.* Essex: Pearson Education.

DESTATIS (2016). Genesis Online Database.
[https://www-genesis.destatis.de/genesis/online/data;jsessionid=F7951A5E8D41F
469AC5BFADA513F3E9F.tomcat_GO_1_1?operation=abruftabelleBearbeiten
&levelindex=1&levelid=1449082731467&auswahloperation=abruftabelleAuspra
egungAuswaehlen&auswahlverzeichnis=ordnungsstruktur&auswahlziel=werte
abruf&selectionname=12411-0006&auswahltext=%23Z-31.12.2014%23SALT013-
ALT022%2CALT021%2CALT043%2CALT020%2CALT042%2CALT019%2CALT041
%2CALT023%2CALT036%2CALT035%2CALT034%2CALT018%2CALT040%2CAL
T017%2CALT039%2CALT016%2CALT038%2CALT015%2CALT037%2CALT049%2
CALT033%2CALT044%2CALT032%2CALT031%2CALT030%2CALT048%2CALT0-
47%2CALT046%2CALT045%2CALT025%2CALT024%2CALT029%2CALT028%2C
ALT027%2CALT026&nummer=5&variable=2&name=GES&werteabruf=Werteabr
uf] Accessed 08 August 2016.

DEUTSCHE BANK RESEARCH (2011). *Textil-/Bekleidungsindustrie: Innovation und
Internationalisierung als Erfolgsfaktoren.* [https://www.dbresearch.de/PROD/
DBR_INTERNET_DE-PROD/PROD0000000000275049.pdf] Accessed 14 June 2016.

DEUTSCHES GLOBAL COMPACT NETZWERK (2014). *Leitprinzipien für Wirtschaft und Menschen-
rechte.* [https://www.globalcompact.de/wAssets/docs/Menschenrechte/Publika-
tionen/leitprinzipien_fuer_wirtschaft_und_menschenrechte.pdf]
Accessed 03 June 2016.

DEUTSCHES INSTITUT FÜR NORMIERUNG (2016). *DIN – kurz erklärt.* [http://www.din.de/de/
uebernormen-und-standards/basiswissen] Accessed 21 June 2016.

DEUTSCHES INSTITUT FÜR NORMIERUNG (2016A). *DIN e.V.*
[http://www.din.de/de/din-und-seine-partner/din-e-v] Accessed 21 June 2016.

DEVINNEY, T., AUGER, P. & ECKHARDT, G. (2010). *The myth of the ethical consumer.*
Cambridge: Cambridge University Press.

D'HEUR, M. (2015). Shared.value.chain – Profitables Wachstum durch nachhaltig gemeinsame Wertschöpfung. In A. Schneider & R. Schmidpeter (Eds.), *Corporate Social Responsibility* (pp. 339-357). Heidelberg: Springer Gabler.

DIEKMANN, A. (2005). Empirische Sozialforschung. Reinbek bei Hamburg: Rowohlt.

DRUCKER, P. (1984): The New Meaning of Corporate Social Responsibility, in: *California Management Review*, (26)2, 53-63.

DUONG DINH, H. (2010). *Corporate Social Responsibility* (Doctoral dissertation). Wiesbaden: Gabler Verlag.

EBERL, M. (2006). *Unternehmensreputation und Kaufverhalten* (Doctoral dissertation). Wiesbaden: Deutscher Universitätsverlag.

EGAN, D. (2010). Retail sector. In W. Visser, D. Matten, M. Pohl & N. Tolhurst (Eds.): *The A to Z of Corporate Social Responsibility*, (pp. 344-346). West Sussex: John Wiley & Sons.

EINWILLER, S. (2014). Reputation und Image: Grundlagen, Einflussmöglichkeiten, Management. In A. Zerfaß & M. Piwinger (Eds.): *Handbuch Unternehmens-kommunikation*, (pp. 371-391). Wiesbaden: Springer Gabler.

EISENEGGER, M. & SCHRANZ, M. (2011). CSR – Moralisierung des Reputationsmanagements. In J. Raupp, S. Jarolimek & F. Schultz (Eds.): *Handbuch CSR*, (pp. 71-96). Wiesbaden: VS Verlag.

EISENEGGER, M. & SCHRANZ, M. (2011A). Reputation Management and Corporate Social Responsibility. In O. Ihlen, J. Bartlett, S. May (Eds.), *The Handbook of Communication and Corporate Social Responsibility*, (pp. 87-109). West Sussex: John Wiley & Sons.

ELKINGTON, J. (1998). *Cannibals with forks: the triple bottom line of 21st century business.* Oxford: Capstone.

ELKINGTON, J. (2007). Corporate Sustainability. In W. Visser, D. Matten, M. Pohl & N. Tolhurst (Eds.): *The A to Z of Corporate Social Responsibility,* (pp. 132-139). West Sussex: John Wiley & Sons.

ENGELHARDT, A. (2012). *Schwarzbuch Baumwolle: Was wir wirklich auf der Haut tragen.* Wien: Deuticke im Paul Zsolnay Verlag.

ENVIRONMENTAL JUSTICE FOUNDATION (2007). The deadly chemicals in cotton. [http://www.pan-uk.org/attachments/125_the_deadly_chemicals_in_cotton_part1.pdf] Accessed 04 June 2016.

EULER HERMES ECONOMIC RESEARCH (2014). *Textil und Bekleidung in Deutschland: Eine Branche mit zwei Gesichtern.* [http://www.eulerhermes.de/mediacenter/Lists /mediacenter-documents/euler-hermes-branchenbericht-textilindustrie-deutsch land.pdf] Accessed 15 June 2016.

EUROPÄISCHE KOMMISSION (2011). *Eine neue EU-Strategie (2011-14) für die soziale Ver- antwortung der Unternehmen (CSR).* [http://eurlex.europa.eu/LexUriServ/LexUri Serv.do?uri=COM:2011:0681:FIN:DE:PDF] Accessed 03 June 2016.

EUROPÄISCHE KOMMISSION (2016). *Offenlegung nichtfinanzieller Informationen.* [http://ec.europa.eu/finance/company-reporting/non-financial_reporting/ index_de.htm] Accessed 24 May 2016.

FABER-WIENER, G. (2015). CSR und Kommunikation – praktische Zugänge. In A. Schneider & R. Schmidpeter (Eds.), *Corporate Social Responsibility,* (pp. 750-766). Heidelberg: Springer Gabler.

FAULBAUM, F., PRÜFER, P. & REXROTH, M. (2009). *Was ist eine gute Frage?* Wiesbaden: VS.

FIFKA, M. (2015). Zustand und Perspektiven der Nachhaltigkeitsberichterstattung. In A. Schneider & R. Schmidpeter (Eds.), *Corporate Social Responsibility* (pp. 835-848). Heidelberg: Springer Gabler.

FIFKA, M. & LOZA ADAUI, C. (2015). Corporate Social Responsibility (CSR) Reporting – Administrative Burden or Competitive Advantage? In L. O'Riordan, P. Zmuda & S. Heinemann (Eds.), *New Perspectives on Corporate Social Responsibility* (pp. 285-300). Wiesbaden: Springer Fachmedien.

FLEISCHER, A. (2015). *Reputation und Wahrnehmung* (Doctoral dissertation). Wiesbaden: Springer Fachmedien.

FLETCHER, K. (2014). *Sustainable Fashion and Textiles.* Oxon, UK: Routledge.

FLICK, U. (2008). *Triangulation.* Wiesbaden: VS.

FLICK, U. (2011). *Triangulation.* Wiesbaden: VS.

FLICK, U. (2014). *Qualitiative Sozialforschung.* Reinbek bei Hamburg: Rohwolt.

FREEMAN, R., HARRISON, J., WICKS, A., PARMAR, B., DE COLLE, S. (2010). *Stakeholder Theory.* Cambridge: Cambridge University Press.

GAINES-ROSS, L. (2008). *Corporate Reputation.* New Jersey: John Wiley & Sons.

GASTINGER, K. & GAGGL, P. (2015). CSR als strategischer Managementansatz. In A. Schneider & R. Schmidpeter (Eds.), *Corporate Social Responsibility* (pp. 283-298). Heidelberg: Springer Gabler.

GESIS (2016). *Survey Design and Methodolgy.* [http://www.gesis.org/das-institut/wissen schaftliche-abteilungen/survey-design-and-methodology/] Accessed 13 June 2016.

GFK (2010). *Anteil der Kaufkraft der Deutschen nach Altersgruppen.*
[http://de.statista.com/statistik/daten/studie/163248/umfrage/kaufkraft-nach-altersgruppen/] Access-ed 19 May 2016.

GLÄSER, J. & LAUDEL, G. (2010). *Experteninterviews und qualitative Inhaltsanalyse.*
Wiesbaden: VS.

GLOBAL COMPACT (2016). *Die zehn Prinzipien des global Compact.*
[https://www.globalcompact.de/de/ueber-uns/Dokumente-Ueber-uns/DIE-ZEHN-PRINZIPIEN-1.pdf] Accessed 03 June 2016.

GLOBAL REPORTING INITIATIVE (2016). *G4 Sustainability Reporting Guidelines.* [https://www.globalreporting.org/standards/g4/Pages/default.aspx] Accessed 26 May 2016.

GÖRITZ, A. (2003). Online-Panels. In A. Theobald, M. Dreyer & T. Starsetzki (Eds.), *Online-Marktforschung* (pp. 227-240). Wiesbaden: Gabler.

GOTTSCHALK, P. (2011). *Corporate social responsibility, governance and corporate reputation.* Singapore: World Scientific Publishing.

GRIES, T. (2006). *Textiltechnik? Textiltechnik. Textiltechnik!* Paderborn: Ferdinand Schöningh.

GRIES, T., VEIT, D. & WULFHORST, B. (2014). *Textile Fertigungsverfahren.* München: Carl Hanser.

GRÖMLING, M. & MATTHES, J. (2003). *Globalisierung und Strukturwandel der deutschen Textil- und Bekleidungsindustrie.* Köln: Deutscher Instituts-Verlag.

HAAS, H. & ZADEMACH, H. (2005). Internationalisierung im Textil- und Bekleidungs-gewerbe. *Geographische Rundschau,* (57)2, 30-38.

HACKL, O. (2015). Thesen zu Grenzen von CSR im Handel. In M. Knoppe (Ed.): *CSR und Retail Management* (pp. 92-106). Heidelberg: Springer Gabler.

HANSEN, U. & KRULL, S. (1994). Öko-Label als umweltbezogenes Informationsinstrument: Begründungszusammenhänge und Interessen. *Marketing: Zeitschrift für Forschung,* (16)4, 265-274.

HARTLIEB, B., KIEHL, P. & MÜLLER, N. (2009). *Normierung und Standardisierung.* Berlin: Beuth.

HAUPTMANNS, P. & LANDER, A. (2003). Zur Problematik von Internet-Stichproben. In A. Theobald, M. Dreyer & T. Starsetzki (Eds.), *Online-Marktforschung* (pp. 27-40). Wiesbaden: Gabler.

HEINRICH, P. (2013). CR-Kommunikation – die Instrumente. In P. Heinrich (Ed.), *CSR und Kommunikation* (pp. 79-102). Heidelberg: Springer Gabler.

HEINRICH, P. & SCHMIDPETER, R. (2013). Wirkungsvolle CSR-Kommunikation – Grundlagen. In P. Heinrich (Ed.), *CSR und Kommunikation* (pp. 1-25). Heidelberg: Springer Gabler.

HELL, P. (2009). *Türkische Textilfabriken: Tödlicher Sand in der Jeans-Maschine.* [http://www.spiegel.de/panorama/gesellschaft/tuerkische-textilfabriken-toedlicher-sand-in-der-jeans-maschine-a-614541.html] Accessed 18 June 2016.

HERGER, N. (2006). *Vertrauen und Organisationskommunikation.* Wiesbaden: VS Verlag.

HESSNATUR (2016). hessnatur. [http://www.hessnatur.com/de/] Accessed 01 August 2016.

HESSNATUR (2016A). *40 Jahre responsible Innovation.* [http://www.hessnatur.com/de/meilensteine?contentID=homepage] Accessed 01 August 2016.

HOLDINGHAUSEN, H. (2015). *Dreimal anziehen, weg damit.* Frankfurt/Main: Westend Verlag.

HUCK-SANDHU, S. (2011). Corporate Social Responsibility und internationale Public Relations. In J. Raupp, S. Jarolimek & F. Schultz (Eds.): *Handbuch CSR,* (pp. 205-228). Wiesbaden: VS Verlag.

HUWART, J. & VERDIER, L. (2014). *Die Globalisierung der Wirtschaft.*
[http://www.oecd-ilibrary.org/docserver/download/0111115e.pdf?expires=14615
86675&id=id&accname=guest&checksum=7C17A3B163F40C61E75062A44FE103EF]
Accessed 25 May 2016.

IFH INSTITUT FÜR HANDELSFORSCHUNG GMBH (2012). *20 Jahre Oeko-Tex Standard 100.*
[https://www.oeko-ex.com/media/downloads/OETS_100_Consumer_Survey
2012_de.pdf] Accessed 24 July 2016.

IHLEN, O., BARTLETT, J. & MAY, S. (2011). Corporate Social Reponsibility and
Communication. In O. Ihlen, J. Bartlett, S. May (Eds.), *The Handbook of Com-
munication and Corporate Social Responsibility,* (pp. 3-22). West Sussex:
John Wiley & Sons.

INTERNATIONALES ARBEITSAMT (2006). *Dreigliedrige Grundsatzerklärung über multinationale Unternehmen und Sozialpolitik.* [http://www.ilo.org/wcmsp5/groups/
public/---ed_emp/---emp_ent/documents/publication/wcms_179118.pdf]
Accessed 03 June 2016.

IVEY, P. (2007). Reputation. In W. Visser, D. Matten, M. Pohl & N. Tolhurst (Eds.):
The A to Z of Corporate Social Responsibility, (pp. 390-392). West Sussex: John
Wiley & Sons.

IVEY, P. (2007A). Licence to operate. In W. Visser, D. Matten, M. Pohl & N. Tolhurst (Eds.):
*The A to Z of Corporate Social Responsibility, (*pp. 311-312). West Sussex: John
Wiley & Sons.

IVEY, P. (2007B). Greenwash. In W. Visser, D. Matten, M. Pohl & N. Tolhurst (Eds.):
The A to Z of Corporate Social Responsibility, (pp. 248). West Sussex: John Wiley
& Sons.

JAROLIMEK, S. (2014). CSR-Kommunikation: Zielsetzungen und Erscheinungsformen.
In A. Zerfaß & M. Piwinger (Eds.): *Handbuch Unternehmenskommunikation,*
(pp. 1269-1283). Wiesbaden: Springer Gabler.

JAROLIMEK, S. & RAUPP, J. (2011). Zur Inhaltsanalyse von CSR-Kommunikation. In J. Raupp, S. Jarolimek & F. Schultz (Eds.): *Handbuch CSR,* (pp. 497-516). Wiesbaden: VS Verlag.

JASCH, C. (2015). CSR und Berichterstattung. In A. Schneider & R. Schmidpeter (Eds.), *Corporate Social Responsibility,* (pp. 823-834). Heidelberg: Springer Gabler.

JONKER, J. (2015). The future of Corporate Social Responsibility: Towards an ecology of Organisations focused on sustainability. In L. O'Riordan, P. Zmuda & S. Heinemann (Eds.): *New Perspectives on Corporate Social Responsibility* (pp. 23-47). Wiesbaden: Springer Fachmedien.

KERSTEN, C. (2012). *Nachhaltigkeitsstandards und Wettbewerbsstrategien in der textilen Kette am Beispiel des GOTS* (Unpublished master's thesis). Leuphana Universität, Lüneburg.

KIRCHHOFF, S., KUHNT, S., LIPP, P. & SCHLAWIN, S. (2010). *Der Fragebogen.* Wiesbaden: VS.

KLEINALTENKAMP, M. (1993). *Standardisierung und Marktprozeß.* Wiesbaden: Gabler.

KOHN, B. (2009). *Türkei verbietet das Sandstrahlen von Jeans.* [http://www.br.de/radio /bayern2/wissen/kalenderblatt/2703-jeans-sandstrahlen-staublunge100.html] Accessed 18 May 2016.

KOTLER, P. & KELLER, K. (2012). *Marketing Management.* Boston: Pearson.

KOTLER, P., KELLER, K. & BLIEMEL F. (2007). *Marketing-Management.* München: Pearson.

KOTLER, P., KELLER, K. & OPRESNIK, M. (2015). *Marketing Management.* Hallbergmoos: Pearson.

KOTLER, P., KELLER, K., HASSAN, S., BAALBAKI, I. & SHAMMA, H. (2012). *Marketing Management.* Essex: Pearson.

KPMG (2011). *KPMG International Survey of Corporate Responsibility Reporting 2011.*
[https://www.kpmg.com/GR/en/IssuesAndInsights/ArticlesPublications/Sustai
nability/Documents/ss-KPMG-International-Survey-of-CR-Reporting-2011-Nov-
2011-web.pdf] Accessed 26 May 2016.

KPMG (2013). The KPMG Survey of Corporate Responsibility Reporting 2013.
[https://www.kpmg.com/Global/en/IssuesAndInsights/ArticlesPublications/
corporate-responsibility/Documents/corporate-responsibility-reporting-survey-
2013-exec-summary.pdf] Accessed 25 May 2016.

KUTSCH, H. (2007). *Repräsentativität in der Online-Marktforschung* (Doctoral dissertation).
Köln: Josef Eul.

LEITHERER, E. (1994). Die Geschichte der Markierung und des Markenwesens.
In M. Bruhn (Ed.): *Handbuch Markenartikel*, (pp. 135-152).
Stuttgart: Schäffer-Poeschel.

LUO, X. & BHATTACHARYA, C. (2006). *Corporate Social Responsibility, Customer Satisfaction,
and Market Value.* [http://www.fox.temple.edu/cms/wp-content/upload/2013
/09/jm-csr-oct06.pdf] Accessed 24 May 2016.

LUX, W. (2012). Innovationen im Handel. Heidelberg: Springer Gabler.

LUX, W. (2013). CSR-Kommunikation im Handel. In P. Heinrich (Ed.),
CSR und Kommunikation (pp. 133-145). Heidelberg: Springer Gabler.

MARTINS, L. (2005). A model of the effects of reputational rankings on organizational
change. *Organization Science,* (16)6, 701-720.

MAST, C. & FIEDLER, K. (2007). Nachhaltige Unternehmenskommunikation. In G. Michelsen
& J. Godemann: *Handbuch Nachhaltigkeitskommunikation*, (pp. 567-578).
München: oekom.

MAST, C. (2010). *Unternehmenskommunikation.* Stuttgart: Lucius & Lucius.

MAST, C. (2013). *Unternehmenskommunikation.* Konstanz und München: UVK.

MAY, S. (2011). Organizational Communication and Corporate Social Responsibility. In O. Ihlen, J. Bartlett, S. May (Eds.), *The Handbook of Communication and Corporate Social Responsibility,* (pp. 87-109). West Sussex: John Wiley & Sons.

MAYRING, P. (2002). *Qualitative Sozialforschung.* Weinheim: Beltz.

MAYRING, P. (2003). *Qualitative Inhaltsanalyse.* Weinheim: Beltz.

MCINTOSH, M. (2007). Corporate Citizenship. In W. Visser, D. Matten, M. Pohl, & N. Tolhurst (Eds.): *The A to Z of Corporate Social Responsibility,* (pp. 97-102). West Sussex: John Wiley & Sons.

MIRVIS, P. (2011). Reputation and Corporate Social Responsibility: A Global View. In R. Burke, G. Martin, & Cary Cooper (Eds.), *Corporate Reputation,* (pp. 89-110). Surrey: Gower Publishing Limited.

MÖLLER, V., KOEHLER, D., & STUBENRAUCH, I. (2015). Finding the Value in Environmental, Social, and Governance Performance. In L. O'Riordan, P. Zmuda, S. Heinemann (Eds.), *New Perspectives on Corporate Social Responsibility,* (pp. 276-283). Wiesbaden: Springer Gabler.

MÜNSTERMANN, M. (2007). *Corporate Social Responsibility* (Doctoral dissertation). Wiesbaden: Gabler.

NIELSEN (2015). *Soziales Engagement, ja bitte! Doch Qualität und Leistung gehen vor.* [http://www.nielsen.com/de/de/insights/reports/2015/Social-Responsibility.html] Accessed 20 July 2016.

NUGGETS MARKET RESEARCH AND CONSULTING (2015). *Greenpeace – Usage & Attitude Mode unter Jugendlichen.* [http://www.greenpeace.de/sites/ www.greenpeace.de/files/ publications/mode-unter-jugendlichen-greenpeace-umfrage.pdf] Accessed 16 June 2016.

OECD (2011). *OECD-Leitsätze für multinationale Unternehmen.* [http://www.oecd. org/
corporate/mne/48808708.pdf] Accessed 03 June 2016.

OLIVER, R. (1999). Whence Consumer Loyalty? *Journal of Marketing,*
(63)Special Issue 1999, 33-44.

OLIVER, R. (2010). *Satisfaction: A behavioural perspective on the consumer.* New York:
M.E. Sharpe.

O'RIORDAN, L. & ZMUDA, P. (2015). Conceptual Framework for Corporate Responsibility
Management: A Critical Review of Sustainable Business Practice Based on a
Case Study of a Leading Transnational Corporation. In L. O'Riordan, P. Zmuda,
S. Heinemann (Eds.), *New Perspectives on Corporate Social Responsibility,*
(pp. 473-504). Wiesbaden: Springer Gabler.

O'RIORDAN, L., ZMUDA, P. & HEINEMANN, S. (2015). Foreword. In L. O'Riordan, P. Zmuda,
S. Heinemann (Eds.), *New Perspectives on Corporate Social Responsibility,*
(pp. V-VI). Wiesbaden: Springer Gabler.

OTTO (2013). *Lebensqualität: Otto Group Trendstudie 2013 - Vierte Studie zum ethischen
Konsum.* [http://trendbuero.com/wp-content/uploads/2013/12/Trendbuero_Otto_
Group_Trendstudie_2013.pdf] Accessed 26 May 2016.

PIWINGER, M. (2014). Das Reputationsrisiko: Herausforderungen und Bedeutung für die
Unternehmensführung. In A. Zerfaß & M. Piwinger (Eds.): *Handbuch Unternehmenskommunikation,* (pp. 307-327). Wiesbaden: Springer Gabler.

PLEIL, T. (2012). Kommunikation in der digitalen Welt. In A. Zerfaß & T. Pleil (Eds.):
Handbuch Online-PR, (pp. 17-38). Konstanz: UVK.

PORTER, M. & KRAMER, M. (2002). *The Competitive Advantage of Corporate Philanthropy.*
[https://hbr.org/2002/12/the-competitive-advantage-of-corporate-philanthropy]
Accessed 23 May 2016.

PORTER, M & KRAMER, M. (2006). *Strategy and society: The link between competitive advantage and corporate social responsibility.* [https://hbr.org/2006/12/strategy-and-society-the-link-between-competitive-advantage-and-corporate-social-responsibility] Accessed 25 May 2016.

POTOCKI, Z. (2015). Altruism as a missing concept in economic rationality: the need for multi-disciplinary perspective. In L. O'Riordan, P. Zmuda, S. Heinemann (Eds.), *New Perspectives on Corporate Social Responsibility,* (pp. 127-146). Wiesbaden: Springer Gabler.

POYNTER, R. (2010). *The Handbook of Online and Social Media Research.* West Sussex: John Wiley & Sons.

RAPOPORT, N. & DHARAN, B. (2004). *Enron: Corporate Fiascos and Their Implications.* New York: Foundation Press.

RAUPP, J. (2011). Die Legitimation von Unternehmen in öffentlichen Diskursen. In J. Raupp, S. Jarolimek, & F. Schultz (Eds.): *Handbuch CSR,* (pp. 97-114). Wiesbaden: VS Verlag.

RAUPP, J., JAROLIMEK, S, & SCHULTZ, F. (2011). Glossar. In J. Raupp, S. Jarolimek, & F. Schultz (Eds.): *Handbuch CSR,* (pp. 519-528). Wiesbaden: VS Verlag.

RESPONDI (2016). Access panels. [http://www.respondi.com/de/access-panels-leistungen#ACCESSPANELS] Accessed 13 June 2016.

RESPONDI (2016A). Online samples and online panels. [http://www.respondi.com/wp-content/uploads/2014/06/DE_OurAnswersToThe28ESOMARQuestions.pdf] Accessed 13 June 2016.

SABAPATHY, J. (2007). Ethical consumption. In W. Visser, D. Matten, M. Pohl, & N. Tolhurst (Eds.): *The A to Z of Corporate Social Responsibility,* (pp. 195-198). West Sussex: John Wiley & Sons.

SCHERER, A. (2007). Sweatshops. In W. Visser, D. Matten, M. Pohl, & N. Tolhurst (Eds.):
The A to Z of Corporate Social Responsibility, (pp. 451-452). West Sussex: John
Wiley & Sons.

SCHIEBEL, W. (2015). CSR und Marketing. In A. Schneider & R. Schmidpeter (Eds.),
Corporate Social Responsibility, (pp. 705-720). Heidelberg: Springer Gabler.

SCHMIDPETER, R. (2015). Vorwort des Reihenherausgebers: Handel als Dienstleister für eine
nachhaltige Gesellschaft. In M. Knoppe (Ed.): *CSR und Retail Management* (pp.
VII-VIII). Heidelberg: Springer Gabler.

SCHNEIDER, A. (2003). Internationalisierungsstrategien in der deutschen Textil- und
Bekleidungsindustrie - eine empirische Untersuchung (Doctoral dissertation).
[http://publications.rwth-aachen.de/record/61937/files/03_159.pdf]
Accessed 15 June 2016.

SCHNEIDER, A. (2015). Reifegradmodell CSR – eine Begriffsklärung und –abgrenzung. In
A. Schneider & R. Schmidpeter (Eds.), *Corporate Social Responsibility,*
(pp. 21-42). Heidelberg: Springer Gabler.

SCHULZ, O. (2015). Nachhaltige ganzheitliche Werschöpfungskette. In A. Schneider &
R. Schmidpeter (Eds.), *Corporate Social Responsibility,* (pp. 325-338). Heidelberg:
Springer Gabler.

SEN, S. & BHATTACHARYA, C. (2001). Does doing good always lead to doing better?
Consumer reactions to corporate social responsibility.
[https://faculty.fuqua.duke.edu/~moorman/Marketing-Strategy-Seminar-2015/
Session%2012/Sen%20and%20Bhattacharya%202001.pdf] Accessed 25 May 2016.

SEN, S., DU, S. & BHATTACHARYA, C. (2009). Building brand relationship through corporate
social responsibility. In D. MacInnis, C. Park, & J. Priester (Eds.): Handbook of
brand relationships, (pp. 195-211), New York: M.E. Sharpe.

SPIEGEL (2015). Wie häufig kaufen sich (Frauen) im Allgemeinen für sich persönlich Kleidung? [http://de.statista.com/statistik/daten/studie/437661/umfrage/umfrage-unter-frauen-in-deutschland-zur-haeufigkeit-des-kaufs-von-kleidung/] Accessed 19 May 2016.

SPIEGEL (2015A). Wie häufig kaufen Sie (Männer) im Allgemeinen für sich persönlich Kleidung? [http://de.statista.com/statistik/daten/studie/437732/umfrage/umfrag-unter-ma ennern-in-deutschland-zur-haeufigkeit-des-kaufs-von-kleidung/] Accessed 19 May 2016.

STARMANNS, M. (2010). "Corporate Responsibility" in der Modeindustrie. *Geographische Rundschau*, 4, 26-33.

STATISTA (2016). Prognostizierte Umsatzentwicklung in der Textil- und Bekleidungs-industrie in Deutschland in den Jahren von 2007 bis 2020 (in Milliarden Euro). [de.statista.com/statistik/daten/studie/248640/umfrage/prognose-zum-umsatz-in-der-textil-und-bekleidungsindustrie-in-deutschland/] Accessed 20 May 2016.

STIFTUNG WARENTEST (2011). Jeans CSR: Viele Anbieter mauern. [https://www.test.de/Jeans-CSR-Viele-Anbieter-mauern-4281449-4281455/] Accessed 18. May 2016.

STOCKI, R. & LAPOT, A. (2015). Vroom's Participation Model as a Foundation of Organisation Audit: A new Approach to CSR. In L. O'Riordan, P. Zmuda, S. Heinemann (Eds.), *New Perspectives on Corporate Social Responsibility*, (pp. 191-212). Wiesbaden: Springer Gabler.

STOWASSER, J. (1960). *Der kleine Stowasser.* München: G. Freitag.

SUE, V. & RITTER, L. (2012). *Conducting Online Surveys.* Thousand Oaks: SAGE Publications.

THEOBALD, E. & NEUNDORFER, L. (2010). *Qualitative Online-Marktforschung.* Baden-Baden: Nomos Verlagsgesellschaft.

THEOBALD, A. (2014). *Handbuch Online-Marktforschung.* Norderstedt: Books on Demand.

TRIGEMA (2012). Trigema TV-spot. [https://www.youtube.com/watch?v=4v2lSOZpR98] Accessed 23 July 2016.

UMWELTBUNDESAMT (2016). REACH – Registration, evaluation, authorisation and restriction of chemicals. [http://www.reach-info.de] Accessed 26 July 2016.

VISSER, W. (2007). Sustainability. In W. Visser, D. Matten, M. Pohl, & N. Tolhurst (Eds.): *The A to Z of Corporate Social Responsibility,* (pp. 445-446). West Sussex: John Wiley & Sons.

VISSER, W. (2011). *The age of responsibility.* West Sussex: John Wiley & Sons.

VISSER, W. (2013). *Corporate Sustainability & Responsibility.* London: Kaleidoscope Futures.

VOGLER, T. & GRASSER, K. (2015). Entwicklungschancen von Fair-Trade-Produkten im deutschen Lebensmitteleinzelhandel. In M. Knoppe (Ed.): *CSR und Retail Management,* (pp. 149-168). Heidelberg: Springer Gabler.

VRIES, DE H. (2010). *Standardization.* Boston: Kluwer Academic Publishers.

VUMA (ARBEITSGEMEINSCHAFT VERBRAUCHS- UND MEDIENANALYSE) (2015). Beliebteste Bekleidungsgeschäfte und Textilkaufhäuser (Einkauf in den letzten 6 Monaten) in Deutschland von 2012 bis 2015. [http://de.statista.com/statistik/daten/studie/171497/umfrage/in-den-letzten-6-monaten-besuchte-bekleidungsgeschaefte/] Accessed 15 July 2016.

WAGNER, R. & EICHHORN, M. (2013). CSR Kommunikation & Social Media. In P. Heinrich (Ed.): *CSR und Kommunikation,* (pp. 103-117). Heidelberg: Springer Gabler.

WEBER, A. (2015). Nachhaltigkeit und CSR in der Bankenwirtschaft. In A. Schneider & R. Schmidpeter (Eds.), *Corporate Social Responsibility,* (pp. 935-947). Heidelberg: Springer Gabler.

WERNER, M., WELKER, A., & SCHOLZ, J. (2005). *Online Research.* Heidelberg: dpunkt.

WESTERMANN, A. & SCHMID, M. (2012). Public Relations: Online-Kommunikation und Reputationsmanagement im gesellschaftlichen Umfeld. In A. Zerfaß & T. Pleil (Eds.): *Handbuch Online-PR,* (pp. 173-184). Konstanz: UVK.

WILLERSHAUSEN, F. (2012). Die Modelüge – wie deutsche Firmen produzieren lassen. [http://www.wiwo.de/unternehmen/industrie/textilindustrie-die-modeluege-wie-deutsche-firmen-produzieren-lassen/7162224.html] Accessed 16 June 2016.

WILLIAMSON, H. (2014). Kinderarbeit auf den Feldern. [http://www.fr-online.de/politik/menschenrechte-in-usbekistan-kinderarbeit-auf-den-feldern,1472596,29404172.Html] Accessed 20 June 2016.

WILLMROTH, J. (2012). Umfrage: 82 Prozent kennen kein nachhaltiges Unternehmen. [http://green.wiwo.de/umfrage-82-prozent-kennen-kein-nachhaltiges-unternehmen/] Accessed 18 May 2016.

WITTKÖTTER, M. & STEFFEN, M. (2002). Customer Value als Basis des CRM. In D. Ahlert, J. Becker, R. Kanckstedt, & M. Wunderlich (Eds.), *Customer Relationship Management im Handel,* (pp. 73-83). Berlin: Springer-Verlag.

WOLTER, F. (2012). *Heikle Fragen in Interviews* (Doctoral dissertation). Wiesbaden: Springer VS.

WOOD, D. (2007). Corporate Social Responsiveness. In W. Visser, D. Matten, M. Pohl, & N. Tolhurst (Eds.): *The A to Z of Corporate Social Responsibility,* (pp. 131-132). West Sussex: John Wiley & Sons.

WORLD COMMISSION ON ENVIRONMENT AND DEVELOPMENT (1987). Our common future. Oxford: Oxford University Press.

ZERBACK, S. (2015). Kaufkraft ohne Moral. [http://www.deutschlandfunk.de/konsumverhal
ten-von-jugendlichen-kaufkraft-ohne-moral.724.de.html?dram:article_id=327063]
Accessed 30 June 2016.

ZDHC (ZERO DISCHARGE OF HAZARDOUS CHEMICALS PROGRAMME) (2015). Manufacturing
restricted substances list. [http://www.roadmaptozero.com/fileadmin/pdf/MRSL_
v1_1.pdf] Accessed 25 July 2016.

ZIKMUND, W., BABIN, B., CARR, J. & GRIFFIN, M. (2013). *Business Research Methods.*
Canada: Cengage Learning.

Appendix 1: Online survey questionnaire

Available from [www.nicole-franken.de]

Appendix 2: Results of the online survey

Available from [www.nicole-franken.de]

Appendix 3: Expert interviews

Available from [www.nicole-franken.de]

Appendix 4: Fact sheets eco-labels
Fact sheet: Der Blaue Engel

01. Label	
02. Name / Label Owner	Der Blaue Engel / Federal Ministry for the Environment, Nature Conservation and Nuclear Safety (of Germany)
03. Product Group	More than 12.000 products and services Textile products > Textile clothing and textile accessories comprising at least 90 weight per cent textile fibres > Textile products for interior use (interior textiles) comprising at least 90 weight per cent textile fibres > Fibres, yarns and fabrics as well as textile knitwear (including textile compounds and non-woven fabrics) for use in textile clothing and accessories or interior textiles > Non-textile accessories and applications as components of the above-mentioned products[3]
04. Adressee	B2B / B2C
05. Certification by / Institutional Background	RAL gGmbH / under public law
06. Extent of Environmental Criteria	> Improved environmental standards for the manufacturing process > Avoidance of harmful chemicals in the products[4]
07. Extent of Social Criteria	ILO Core Labour Standards

08. Object of Certification	Textile clothing and textile accessories comprising at least 90 weight per cent textile fibres
09. Type of Certification or Monitoring	Examination by RAL GmbH after self-declaration of the applicant, reports of accredited labs are mandatory
10. Certification Costs	> One-off fee of 250 EUR to process the application for the use of the Blue Angel ecolabel > Processing fee of 150 EUR (plus the statutory level of VAT) is to be paid in each case by the applicant for the conclusion of a contract extension > Yearly fee for the use of the environmental label depends on the annual sales[5]
11. Geographical Range	International
12. Amount of Textile Value Chain Steps	Parts of it, end product
13. Method of Standard Development	Multi-stakeholder process: expert hearing of members from economy, consumer associations and environ-mental associations
14. Amount of Qualified Companies Worldwide	1.500 (as of 28.6.2016)
15. Sources	https://www.blauer-engel.de

3 These are excerpts from the company's website [https://www.blauer-engel.de].
4 IBID.
5 IBID.

Fact sheet: Cradle to Cradle

01. Label	
02. Name / Label Owner	Cradle to Cradle certified / Cradle to Cradle Products Innovation Institute, a non-profit organisation
03. Product Group	Auto & Tyres Baby Building Supply & Materials Fashion & Textiles Health & Beauty Home & Office Supply Interior Design & Furniture Materials for Product Designers Packaging & Paper Toys
04. Adressee	B2B / B2C
05. Certification by / Institutional Background	Product assessments are performed by a qualified independent organization trained by the Institute. Assessment Summary Reports are reviewed by the Institute, which certifies products meeting the Standard requirements, and licenses the use of the Cradle to Cradle Certified™ word and design marks to the product manufacturer. Every two years, manufacturers must demonstrate good faith efforts to improve their products in order to have their products recertified. [6]

---

6 These are excerpts from the company's website [http://www.c2ccertified.org].

06. Extent of Environmental Criteria	**1. Material Health** Knowing the chemical ingredients of every material in a product, and optimizing towards safer materials: > Identify materials as either biological or technical nutrients > Understand how chemical hazards combine with likely exposures to determine potential threats to human health and the environment **2. Material Reutilization** Designing products made with materials that come from and can safely return to nature or industry: > Maximize the percentage of rapidly renewable materials or recycled content used in a product > Maximize the percentage of materials that can be safely reused, recycled, or composted at the product's end of use > Designate your product as technical (can safely return to industry) and/or biological (can safely return to nature) **3. Renewable Energy & Carbon Management** Envisioning a future in which all manufacturing is powered by 100% clean renewable energy: > Source renewable electricity and offset carbon emissions for the product's final manufacturing stage **4. Water Stewardship** Manage clean water as a precious resource and an essential human right: > Address local geographic and industry water impact at each manufacturing facility > Identify, assess and optimize any industrial chemicals in a facility's effluent[7]

---

7 IBID.

07. Extent of Social Criteria	**5. Social Fairness** Design operations to honour all people and natural systems affected by the creation, use, disposal or reuse of a product: > Use globally recognized resources to conduct selfassessments to identify local and supply chain issues and third party audits to assure optimal conditions > Make a positive difference in the lives of employees, and the local community[8]
08. Object of Certification	> Raw Material > Fabrics > Yarn > Thread, Trims and Notions > Dyes and Finishes > Apparel
09. Type of Certification or Monitoring	The Cradle to Cradle Products Innovation Institute evaluates products for certification through a network of assessment bodies who are accredited by the Institute based on the experience, qualifications, and training of organization's staff. Accredited Assessors are trained and accredited to help companies achieve certification for their products.[9] The various assessment bodies are listed on the website of cradle2cradle.
10. Certification Costs	> New Product Certification € 2.000 > Annual Product Certification € 500 > Interim Assessment Review € 500 > Certificate Correction € 80
11. Geographical Range	Worldwide

8 IBID.
9 IBID.

12. Amount of Textile Value Chain Steps	All besides cultivation of fibres
13. Method of Standard Development	Five advisory groups, one for each category of the Cradle to Cradle Certified™ Product Standard, have been formed by the Certifications Standards Board to provide expert guidance[10]
14. Amount of Qualified Companies Worldwide	45 (as of 02.07.2016)
15. Sources	http://www.c2ccertified.org

10 IBID.

Fact sheet: Fairtrade Certified Cotton

01. Label	
02. Name / Label Owner	Fairtrade International / Fairtrade Labelling Organizations International eV (FLO)
03. Product Group	Food and beverages, cotton, gold, flowers, carbon credits, composite products, sports balls
04. Adressee	B2B / B2C
05. Certification by / Institutional Background	FLOCERT as independent specially accredited body of FLO
06. Extent of Environmental Criteria	**Cotton** > Environmentally friendly cultivation > Protection of natural resources > Ban on dangerous pesticides > Ban on genetically modified seeds > Encourage the use of organic methods of cotton growing through subcharges[11] **Textile** > No hazardous substances > No highly hazardous processes > Waste water treatment > Measures to reduce water consumption > Emission control techniques > Measuring reduction of emissions > Energy consumption > Waste collection and separation > Cleaning, storing and disposal of hazardous waste > Measurement and environmental control > Awareness raising on environmental responsibility[12]

07. Extent of Social Criteria	**Cotton**
	> Organisation of democratic communities (for cooperatives)
	> Enhancement of trade union organisations (on plantations)
	> Regulated working conditions
	> Ban on exploitative child labour
	> Ban on discrimination
	> The Fairtrade Minimum Prices for cotton are set at different levels depending on the producing region. The Minimum Prices always cover the costs of sustainable production. Furthermore, if the market price is higher than the Fairtrade Minimum Price, the market price applies
	> Fairtrade Minimum Prices for organic cotton are set 20 percent higher than the Fairtrade conventional Minimum Prices
	> In addition to the Fairtrade price, the buyers must pay a Fairtrade Premium of US$ 5 cents per kilo of Fairtrade seed cotton. This is used by the producer organizations for social and economic investments such as education and health services, processing equipment and loans to members.
	> Evidence of flow of goods and money
	> Guidelines for the use of labels
	> Transparent trade relations
	> Pre-export lines of credit are given to the producer organizations if requested, of up to 60% of the purchase price[13]
	Textile
	> Freedom from Discrimination
	> Freedom from Forced and Compulsory Labour
	> Child Labour and Child Protection – no children under 15 employed
	> Freedom of Association and Collective Bargaining
	> Conditions of Employment: wages, benefits and working hours
	> Occupational Health and Safety[14]

11 These are excerpts from the company's websites [http://www.fairtrade.net] and [https://www.fairtrade-deutschland.de].
12 IBID. | 13 IBID. | 14 IBID. | 15 IBID.

08. Object of Certification	Companies and products
09. Type of Certification or Monitoring	Fairtrade standards are set in accordance with the ISEAL Code of good practice on standard setting; this process involves consultation with stakeholders
10. Certification Costs	Depending on duration, extent and place of certification for farmers; other standards are chargeable
11. Geographical Range	Worldwide
12. Amount of Textile Value Chain Steps	Criteria for the whole textile value chain
13. Method of Standard Development	Decisions about Fairtrade standards are made by the Fairtrade International Standards Committee. The standard setting process is managed by Fairtrade International's Standards unit, which publishes its annual workplan as part of good practices in standards setting. Fairtrade International's Standards & Pricing Unit is in charge of creating new standards and revising existing standards.[15]
14. Amount of Qualified Companies Worldwide	1.226 companies (whole product range); almost 1.45 million farmers were members of Fairtrade small producer or contract production organizations, while 204.000 people worked in Fairtrade certified hired labour organizations. The majority of these workers are on plantations, but there were also almost 5.400 workers in six factories with certification to make Fairtrade soccer balls in Pakistan.[16]
15. Sources	http://www.fairtrade.net https://www.fairtrade-deutschland.de

---

16 These are excerpts from the company's websites [http://www.fairtrade.net] and [https://www.fairtrade-deutschland.de].

Fact sheet: GOTS

01. Label	
02. Name / Label Owner	Global Organic Textile Standard (GOTS) / Global Standard International Working Group, an association of four member organisations: OTA (USA), IVN (Germany), Soil Association (UK), JOCA (Japan)
03. Product Group	Textiles made of organic fibres
04. Adressee	B2B / B2C
05. Certification by / Institutional Background	GOTS International Working Group / private
06. Extent of Environmental Criteria	> At all stages throughout processing, organic fibre products must be separated from conventional fibre products > All chemical inputs (e.g. dyes, auxiliaries and process chemicals) must be evaluated and meet basic requirements on toxicity and biodegradability / eliminability > Prohibition of critical inputs such as toxic heavy metals, formaldehyde, aromatic solvents, functional nano particles, genetically modified organisms (GMO) and their enzymes > The use of synthetic sizing agents is restricted; knitting and weaving oils must not contain heavy metals > Bleaches must be based on oxygen (no chlorine bleaching) > Azo dyes that release carcinogenic amine compounds are prohibited

	> Discharge printing methods using aromatic solvents and plastisol printing methods using phthalates and PVC are prohibited > Restrictions for accessories (e.g. no PVC, nickel or chrome permitted) > All operators must have an environmental policy including target goals and procedures to minimise waste and discharges > Wet processing units must keep full records of the use of chemicals, energy, water consumption and waste water treatment, including the disposal of sludge. The wasted water from all wet processing units must be treated in a functional waste water treatment plant > Packaging material must not contain PVC. Paper or cardboard used in packaging material, hang tags, swing tags etc. must be recycled or certified according to FSC or PEFC Key criteria for fibre production > Organic certification of fibres on basis of recognised international or national standards > Certification of fibres from conversion period is possible if the applicable farming standard permits such certification > A textile product carrying the GOTS label grade 'organic' must contain a minimum of 95% certified organic fibres whereas a product with the label grade 'made with organic' must contain a minimum of 70% certified organic fibres[17]
07. Extent of Social Criteria	Social criteria based on the key norms of the ILO must be met by all processors and manufacturers
08. Object of Certification	> Textiles made from at least 70% certified organic natural fibres > The final products may include, but are not limited to fibre products, yarns, fabrics, clothes and home textiles[18]

17 These are excerpts from the company's websites [www.global-standard.org].
18 IBID.

09. Type of Certification or Monitoring	By independent specially accredited bodies once a year
10. Certification Costs	Beginning with EUR 1.300; licence fee for each calendar year EUR 120
11. Geographical Range	Worldwide
12. Amount of Textile Value Chain Steps	Whole textile chain, beginning with certified organic cultivation of fibres
13. Method of Standard Development	The member organisations of the International Working Group are backed up by stakeholder based decision bodies / technical committees, which has ensured that when integrating their respective existing organic textile standards into the GOTS, views of relevant stakeholders were considered from the beginning. The GOTS approved certification bodies are also actively involved in the GOTS revision process through the 'Certifiers Council'[19]
14. Amount of Qualified Companies Worldwide	3.814 (in 2015)
15. Sources	https://www.global-standard.org

19 These are excerpts from the company's websites [www.global-standard.org].

Fact sheet IVN

01. Label	
02. Name / Label Owner	Internationaler Verband der Naturtextilwirtschaft e. V. (IVN)
03. Product Group	Natural fibre textiles
04. Adressee	B2B / B2C
05. Certification by / Institutional Background	IVN / private
06. Extent of Environmental Criteria	Comparable with the GOTS-criteria. The most important difference with respect to the GOTS-standard is the fact that the surface of a textile product (in other words the actual woven or knitted piece without accessories like zippers, ribbing, interfacing, lining, buttons etc.) must be 100% natural and originate in certified organic cultivation (kbA) or certified organic animal husbandry (kbT).[20]
07. Extent of Social Criteria	Social criteria based on the key norms of the ILO must be met by all processors and manufacturers
08. Object of Certification	The entire supply chain involved in textile manufacturing
09. Type of Certification or Monitoring	By independent specially accredited bodies once a year

10. Certification Costs	Depending on the costs of the certifying body – third party certification
11. Geographical Range	Worldwide
12. Amount of Textile Value Chain Steps	The whole textile value chain
13. Method of Standard Development	A guideline committee develops and maintains the IVN guidelines
14. Amount of Qualified Companies Worldwide	45 (as of 27.06.2016)
15. Sources	http://naturtextil.de http://www.naturtextil.com

20 These are excerpts from the company's websites [http://naturtextil.de and http://www.naturtextil.com].

Fact sheet Textiles Vertrauen nach Öko-Tex Standard 100

01. Label	TEXTILES VERTRAUEN **Schadstoffgeprüfte Textilien** nach Öko-Tex Standard 100
02. Name / Label Owner	International Association for Research and Testing in the Field of Textile Ecology (Oeko-Tex), an alliance of 14 textile and audit companies in Europe and Japan
03. Product Group	Textiles
04. Adressee	B2B / B2C
05. Certification by / Institutional Background	Oeko-Tex / private
06. Extent of Environmental Criteria	> Legally banned and regulated substances, e.g. azo dyes, phthalates, heavy metals such as nickel etc. > Harmful chemicals for which no explicit legal regulation exists (yet), e.g. pesticides or allergenic disperse dyestuffs > Parameters for safeguarding health such as a skin-friendly, pH value and good colour fastness[21]
07. Extent of Social Criteria	None
08. Object of Certification	Raw, semi-finished and finished textile products in every processing stage and for all accessory materials used in the process

---

21 These are excerpts from the company's website [www.oeko-tex.com].

09. Type of Certification or Monitoring	By one of the 16 accredited Oeko-Tex test institutes in Europe and Japan; in Germany and France the certificates are issued by a special Oeko-Tex certification centre
10. Certification Costs	Costs for licensing, monitoring the process and laboratory tests
11. Geographical Range	Worldwide
12. Amount of Textile Value Chain Steps	Apart from ready-to-use products, all textile raw materials and intermediate products from all stages of production
13. Method of Standard Development	By independent textile and test institutes of the Oeko-Tex association
14. Amount of Qualified Companies Worldwide	More than 150.000 certificates have been issued and millions of products have been marked with the Oeko-Tex label
15. Sources	https://www.oeko-tex.com http://www.ci-romero.de/gruenemode-oekotex/

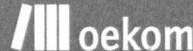
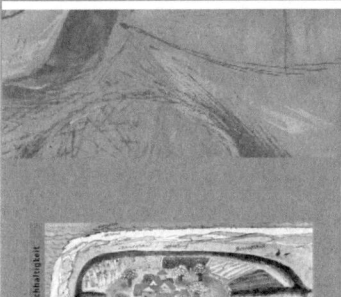

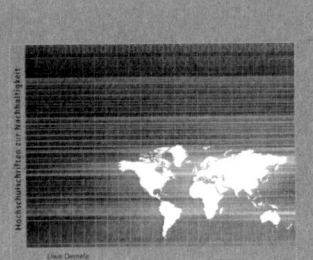

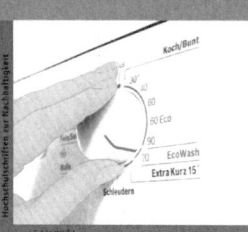
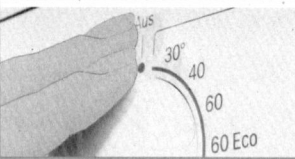